This is 30

Candace R. McClendon

Copyright © 2017 Candace R. McClendon

All rights reserved. All characters appearing in this work are fictitious. Any resemblance to real persons, living or dead, is purely coincidental. No part of this book may be reproduced or transmitted or stored in any form or by any means, electronic or mechanical, including photocopying, recording, or any information storage and retrieval, without permission in writing from the author.

ISBN-13: 978-0692823484

ISBN-10: 0692823484

Publisher: June Jackson Publishing

Library of Congress Control Number: 2016921177

In memory of:
Keith Jackson, Willie C. McClendon, and Robert L. Ficklin.

Introduction

"This is 30". Where did it come from, and how did I, the fictional Queen of all storytelling, decide to write a self-help book? First of all, I really do not consider this a self-help book. The teachings in this book represent my journey. It's the principles that I use to be a better woman, a better person. Do I use them every day? Am I walking around as a Zen Goddess totally unaffected by the world around me? Absolutely not. That is probably the biggest misconception about self-help books. I must admit, that was one of my hesitations to write one. I did not want my audience to assume that I do not have the same struggles that they have, or that I don't have the urge to use profanity when someone crosses me or that I don't catch an attitude when somebody is working my last nerves. I *am* human. I experience all those emotions; however, I have learned how to compartmentalize. I give myself time to feel whatever emotions arise, but then I make a mental habit to try to clear that negative energy from my mind, body, and soul before I go to sleep at night. Does it always work? Nope. But it works most times than not.

And that's the real work. That's how you do the real work. You recognize when something has thrown you off, and you use your teachings, your spiritual persuasion to get back to your center.

What I have learned about women who rarely get back to their center, who rarely address the toxicity in their lives…they may not know they are being toxic. They do not know how to get to their center. They haven't educated themselves on the difference between living from the center opposed to living on the wild side. To clearly define what the wild side is, it is *not* having an over indulgence of adventure, it's being ready to snap every time any little thing doesn't go as planned. It's walking around as if the world is spinning on its axis to accommodate you and all the things you have deemed as important. It's being open to venomous thoughts and relationships. More than anything, it's knowing there's another way to live, but mocking those people who do not live on the wild side because you don't have the courage or know-how to be another way.

"This is 30" addresses those principles that if activated, if used, can help you on your path to discovering how to live your best life. Are they the end all-be all? Of course not, but if anything, the principles will call forth an urge to seek more. Does it only apply to thirty-something year olds? No, I'm in my thirties, so the principles are relatable to me, but I wish I had known these things in my twenties. It's never too early or too late to be a first-rate version of yourself. No to mention, the title is pretty catchy. Hey, it takes a sprinkle of truth and an ounce of creativity to make the world go' round.

Lastly, I challenge you to read with an open mind and read for understanding.

Thank you for being a part of my journey. I am truly walking in my purpose and I totally get that each purchase, each acknowledgement, each mention or share on social media, each "great job" is confirmation that I am walking in God's will, which will ultimately bring me to a new place on my quest for living a fulfilled life. It is my hope that these principles confirm and/or awaken a renewed sense of purpose within you. You are appreciated.

Chapter 1

"If you're not in the parade, you watch the parade. That's Life."

"If you're not in the parade, you watch the parade. That's Life."

~Mike Ditha

Here's the routine:

1. Wake up in the morning.
2. Check Facebook and Instagram.
3. Get ready for work.
4. Drive to work thinking why can't you be like one of those women on Instagram or Facebook that seem to have it all together.
5. Get to work and immediately feel bummed out
6. Roll your eyes at your boss if she thinks you're going to keep doing all this stupid shit for only $10.00 an hour when you know her job better than she know it.
7. Do the extra shit anyway. (Snap Chat your annoyed face)
8. Get off work.
9. Eat.
10. Watch reality television, while thinking… "That damn Nene got it going on, I could be her. She don't have any real talent anyway."
11. Check Facebook and Instagram.
12. Go to Sleep.

If any part of this routine rang true for you, you are clearly on the street watching the parade. Not only are you watching the parade, you are holding out your hand for candy and beads while standing in the same spot hoping that the people in the parade will see you fiercely waving your arms around like a crazy lady. I hate to tell you this, but they don't see you. I mean, how could they? What part of your routine shows a person who is tired of the same ole, same ole? If you do the same thing day in and day out, when will the people in the parade notice you? The bigger question is, when will you notice yourself?

....

Lisa is in her early thirties. She has worked as an Administrative Assistant for the past seven years. Since getting hired at her current job, she has been sent on countless trainings on how to coordinate events, how to create infographics, how to update a fully functioning website, and how to effectively market to the masses on social media. Ideally, Lisa shouldn't have to wear so many hats, but her boss is a cheapskate and she refuses to staff the company with the necessary manpower. Especially since Lisa can do everything, and has shown that she doesn't have a problem doing everything.

Lisa was a top performing student in high school, and finished her Bachelor's degree earning the distinguished honor of Magna Cum Laude. She completed her program in four short years, majoring in Marketing and Advertising; however, this is not how she envisioned her life. After graduating, Lisa just couldn't seem to find her footing. She went on countless interviews, and applied to all types of internships, but they all said the same thing.

"You just don't have enough experience. Earning good grades is one thing, but showing us you know how to apply what you learned is something totally different. Good luck with your search. At this time we have decided to go with another candidate."

Because Lisa has never been one to sit around and do nothing, she eventually got a part-time job at a retail store to hold her over. Several months passed by and she found herself waitressing during the day and folding high-end sweaters at night. The tips were good and she qualified for some awesome discounts at the department store. That kept her family happy. That kept them off her back.

One day, a very sharp dressing woman came into the store, and needed help finding an outfit for her husband. Lisa had a knack for working with people. She learned early on that in order to thrive in retail, you have to have exceptional customer service skills and a love for people. Lisa swooped in and delivered her beaming white smile, perky attitude, and ability to implement her marketing skills by convincing the woman to purchase the whole one thousand dollar suit over just a nice shirt and tie. Needless to say, the woman walked out of the store with the suit and later returned with a job offer to work at an up-and-coming small business.

Lisa was interested and knew God had somehow placed this woman in her life. She quit the retail and waitressing gig, and worked like hell to prove herself to her boss. At first, the woman noticed every little detail. She praised Lisa when she added extra details to reports, she applauded her for staying late, she rewarded her for helping the company to meet goals…but all that stopped after just one year. Lisa found herself clocking in to a list of "to-dos" already stacked on her desk, and more emails opposed to personal contact. It seemed as if the company was doing well and expanding, but Lisa's position wasn't heading anywhere.

Fast forward to seven years later. Lisa is the same Administrative Assistant that she was prior to using her marketing/advertising know-how to help the company land clients, prior to helping the company brand itself on social media networks with over thirty thousand followers respectively, prior to working in the background to help her boss land the title of "Top Forty under Forty: Women You Should Watch Out For". Not to mention, most of the deals her boss was being acknowledged for, Lisa made happen. At first she told herself that it was her job to "assist" the administrator. She blamed herself for going outside of the job description to do extra. I mean, it's not her employer's fault that she willingly did more than what was asked. Well, what about the stuff that *was* asked that had nothing to do with her job responsibilities? What about landing all those clients and not receiving any commission from the deals?

Lisa became resentful. She began to view her job as a career dungeon. She began to view her boss as a selfish bitch. She began to water down herself and her role in the company. She did the bare minimum. She stopped being the self-starter that she once was, she only answered when called upon.

....

Now you may be saying to yourself, *"That's what I would do!"*

But I must ask the question, who is that hurting in the long run? You are changing everything about you that makes you *you* because someone failed to acknowledge or reward your worth. Lisa's boss can easily replace her with someone who is just as eager, enthusiastic, and gullible, but where will that leave Lisa? Once you start diluting your talents and work habits, you are essentially rewiring your brain to be less than who you really are. Nothing you did prior to owning this negative attitude exists anymore. You can't go to a new job and say, *"Sorry I'm not performing today, and I use to be better than who I am today. My old boss screwed me up."* More than likely, your new boss will tell you to hit the door until you gain some self-control.

I tend to wonder if Lisa is more resentful at the fact that she never stepped out on her dream to open her own agency, or if she's mad at herself because she truly did trust the promises her boss made her. Every negative and lasting feeling in your body is connected to you, not someone else. They may have triggered the feeling of disgust, but it's something deeper in you that is keeping it alive. It's your job to be transparent and real with yourself. It's your job to figure out what's making your life heavy, and it's your job to get rid of it.

Let's be clear, being in the parade doesn't mean that you have to be the person calling the shots; your own boss. Entrepreneurship is a great thing, but it may not be for you, it may not have been for Lisa. Lisa may have flourished in her own agency, or she may have flourished if her boss would have promoted her and valued her just a little more.

Being in the parade simply means that you are present in your life, that you are an active contributing member in the comings and goings. If you are not an active contributing member, you are just an observer. Are you one of those people that blame others for your mistakes, or are you someone who accepts responsibility? Are you going through the motions and hating every minute of it, or are you constantly trying to be/do better? It's true with anything, either you are in or out, either you're getting better or worse, either you're in the damn parade or still sitting in the corner waving your arms wildly, hoping to be seen.

Here's to not only being seen, here's to doing something about it. Don't just sit in the back and wait for the candy and beads, walk up to the float and take them.

Chapter 2

"Love with your mouth shut, help without breaking your ass or publicizing it, keep cool but care."

> **"Love with your mouth shut, help without breaking your ass or publicizing it, keep cool but care."**
>
> **~Thomas Pynchon**

I'm not sure if it's human nature to want to be patted on the back or not. Where did we learn that from? Maybe it started in grade school. I can remember being in kindergarten and wanting to get that coveted green light. I can remember wanting my teacher to see that I indeed folded up my mat properly after nap time, and even placed it in my cubby hole correctly. I remember wanting my mother to see that I did not waste food on my cute little skirt, and that I didn't scuff my Mary Jane's during recess. I remember wanting that attention from adults. So I'm not sure if I would have done everything I was supposed to do if I did not receive a prize at the end. I recall wanting to be compensated for doing what I was supposed to be doing… anyway. In that case, it is learned behavior. I'm sure there's some psychological jibber-jabish that supports this notion, but in the aim to keep the reading light-hearted and non-academia, we'll say it's something out there that supports our need to be praised.

But boy oh boy can that get us in trouble. Seriously, going out of our way to seek kudos can put us in a worst position than we would be in if we had never did the "deed" in the first place. Especially in a society that is so over-exposed. The phenomenon that we call social media has completely ripped the lid off what we call privacy, and exposed us to people and things we never knew existed. I mean sure, there are privacy settings and I have the option to not share my life with total strangers. But what about if I text someone whom I trust and they screenshot my message and share it with people without my permission? So I guess technology is the mother bear to social media. Don't get me wrong, I love technology, and I equally love social media. If used properly, technology and social media can introduce you to a world you never knew was out there and create opportunities that you may not have normally had.

....

Catherine is your typical thirty-something year old woman. She has a great job, no kids, an adorable little Yorkie, and lives in a modern cul-de-sac in suburbia USA. Catherine was single during the latter part of her twenties after realizing her college sweetheart wasn't going to marry her. She focused all of her energy on climbing the corporate ladder, and decided to put love on the backburner. But now, now things are different. She's reached executive level at the workplace, she's financially secure, and she has a good group of emotional stakeholders in her life.

Catherine's good friend, Naomi, sets her up with a mutual friend. We'll called him Mr. Wonderful. Mr. Wonderful drives a super jazzy automobile, he has the straightest teeth you or your mama have ever seen, and he has an eight-fifty credit score. Not to mention he believes in romance, being faithful, and marriage and kids. God himself dove out of the Heavens, did a full Hail Mary, and delivered this man to Catherine.

In her free time, Catherine is a social media crackerjack. She loves everything about it. You will never see Catherine without her IPhone in her hand; it's that serious for her. She uses technology for a lot of brilliant things like: she can adjust the air in her room with one push of a button, she can let the garage up and down as she's coming down the block, she can see if her Yorkie is okay by monitoring her home…all from her smart phone. But there are some not-so-brilliant things that Catherine uses her phone for. She stalks all of her former friends to see how well they are doing, she wastes a considerable amount of time during the day thumbing through Facebook, and she documents EVERYTHING. Viewing Catherine's social media profiles is like being attached to her belt buckle every single freaking day. She makes sure to take a selfie every morning, just to tell you *"good morning"*, but don't forget the kissy face. Can I say this? Grown women, please stop kissing your phone screen every morning. If you are a professional, for the love of your career, just stop.

Going back to Mr. Wonderful, he's not on any social media networks except for LinkedIn. It's not like he's a ladies man and has something to hide, he's just not into the hype of it all. He's asked Catherine's friends to speak with her about limiting the "sneak shots" she puts on social media in an effort not to hurt her feelings. You know, pictures of his hands at the restaurant table, pictures of his phone, pictures on the inside of his car (making sure you see that emblem on the headrest), pictures of that magnificent cabana in the back of his house, and even the random "he has his head turned, profile pictures". All of the "sneak shots" seem to be harmless. They seem to be taken without the intention of flaunting the relationship, but let's be real; Catherine wants the people in her vast circle to know that she has somebody. What's wrong with that?

The problem is, Mr. Wonderful isn't into it and Catherine is actually turning him off. He doesn't want his colleagues and mutual friends to know every single move he makes. Despite the overwhelming feelings of like for Catherine, he just can't seem to make her understand that he enjoys mystery, with himself and with his woman.

Catherine also has some issues with being praised. She screenshots all of the "likes" that she gets from Instagram and posts them while thanking the "likers" for "liking". Whew, that's a lot of work! She also brags about all the GoFundMe accounts and nonprofits she supports by posting them and talking about them constantly.

Have you picked up on the problem? Catherine has a need to be praised, patted, acknowledged, and seen. Her need for these things may have caused her relationship with Mr. Wonderful to go sour, and it even portrays her as a person who is all about "look at me, look at me!"

No one knows that Catherine was bulimic as a teenager, no one knows that she watched her mother battle domestic violence her whole life. They don't see that she is proud of her relationship with Mr. Wonderful because she never thought a love like this could exist among African Americans, it was never something she had seen growing up. All she knew was infidelity and violence. They don't see that she supports and publicizes these nonprofits and young girls because she knows what it's like to hate yourself and hate your body. She's attempted suicide more times than she can count, and she wants better for the next girl.

....

Yeah, we don't see that. We see the constant need for attention. Her intentions are gold, but her delivery is off. As women, it's important for us to keep some enigma, some secrecy. If you're in to social media and the wonder of sharing your life with people, there's a way to put it out there…without putting it out there. I've been on social media since about 2009. I'm guilty of posting emotional charged tweets when I first started out. As I stated in the beginning, this is about a journey. I'm more mature and more aware of myself now. Although I am in a happy relationship, I never make my posts about him. For some couples, it works. They tag each other. But for me, I prefer to keep my private life private. I'm not comfortable with social media knowing every time I have an argument, or when my someone special bought me flowers or took me out on a date, because those things are for us.

The need for approval goes beyond technology, it sits in the very core of who you are as a person. Sure we all have a desire to be wanted, and needed, and thought of, and highly regarded but it should not impact who we are or what we do for others because we do not get the praise in return. Meaning, if you do something nice for someone, do it because your heart told you to, not for likes, not for followers, not for accolades.

I've learned that when I am in agreeance with who I am, and I have a true love for myself and how I choose to operate my life, I'm okay with not getting decorated by others. My actions and who I am to people I know, and people that I do not know, is a reflection of me, not to be measured by someone and their inability to recognize who I am to them.

It's okay to share yourself with others (relationships, friendships, charity, etc.), but in the event you do that with the hope of getting something back...you're on the wrong track. I have found that one of my greatest assignments is the ability to give myself away without the hopes of it being mirrored. I give myself away because I am love, I have a divine purpose to help people and leave them better than they were.

The thing to ask yourself is, who are you? What motivates you to do for others? What motivates you to give that little extra? Do you feel yourself pulling back when you do not get the outcome you expected? Do you feel yourself pulling back when people fail to give you credit? Now I'm not saying you should totally go out of your way for an unappreciative person. There's a difference in a person not being appreciative and them just not acknowledging you to the degree that you *expect*. It is your job to figure out what's the driving force behind your actions.

Chapter 3

"You cannot expect to live a positive life if you hang with negative people."

"You cannot expect to live a positive life if you hang with negative people."

~Joel Osteen

I repeat, you cannot expect to live a positive life if you hang around negative people. We all know this, but do we live it? Some people think that their positivity is so strong that it can rub off on the other person. If this is you or your thinking, run fast in the opposite direction of the negative people you spend time with. You cannot change another person, they have to change within themselves. I will say it again in hopes that it resonates somewhere deep…real deep. You cannot change another person, they have to change within themselves.

Motivational speaker Jim Rohn famously said that we are the average of the five people we spend the most time with. That explains a lot. For me, I have a *very* small circle. My circle looks more like a dot. I don't think that I am better than people, nor am I hard to get along with…it's just hard to find people I connect with. When I was younger and more immature, I wanted a lot of friends. Yep, I even wanted about twelve bridesmaids. Today, I can barely count five people who will stand beside me on my special day. The thought doesn't make me sad or squeamish, it means that the women who are selected to stand beside me during such an occasion truly bring vitality to my life; quality over quantity.

....

Rachel is in her late twenties, finishing a Master's degree while working full-time. Rachel is on this new self-empowerment kick. She has started taking up Yoga, meditating in the morning and at night, and even opting for self-help books over the steamy romance novels. She is an active member in Oprah's OWN network, being sure to read all the blogs and watch the Super Soul Sunday episodes before going to church. She is serious about changing for the better. Rachel is enrolled in an MBA program and have high hopes of starting her own cupcake shop when she finishes. She learned how to cook from her mother and grandmother. Cooking is second nature to her, but she always had a special love for baking desserts.

Rachel confides in her friends about her aspirations. They listen, and I guess they are supportive since they taste-test all of her latest recipes, but she oftentimes leave them feeling depleted and unmotivated. Rachel recognizes that her friends aren't exactly headed in the right direction, but they have been friends since barrettes and overalls, and she just can't imagine life without them. They all have a mutual friend who joined the military and dropped them as soon as she started adding stamps to her Passport and dating foreign men. Rachel vowed not to be like her, she wanted to bring their neighborhood friends up to her level, not leave them behind.

On one sunny afternoon, Rachel decides to invite her friends over for a small soiree and a bit of good news. She enlists the help of a classmate who will start her own event management company. The room is completely decked out. Delicious desserts and pastries create an aroma of sweetness and success. Rachel is on cloud nine.

Her friends come in about thirty minutes late and begin to socialize and indulge in the sugared affair. Rachel creates a small circle with their spruced up chairs and tell them that an investor has reached out and that she will be opening her bakery much sooner than she expected. The girls do not seem as excited as she thought they would be. Several of them whisper, *"Good job Rach"*, but go back to talking about the latest, scandalous gossip from their small community.

Rachel decides not to let their drifting moods affect her, she cleans up and rushes home to tell her mother. The conversation goes a little something like this:

"What does he want out of the deal? Who in they right mind going to just give a college student all that money for no reason?"

"Mom, he thinks that I'm good and he sits on the advisory board for the college so he knows that I know how to run a business."

"How does he know you know how to run a business when you don't have a business?"

"I do have a business. I bake for people every day. I may not have an actual store, but I'm made good money so far."

"I just smell trouble. I wouldn't do it. That's why I never left my kitchen. Ain't nobody about to put me in some fancy place and give me all those bills when I can cook fine right here."

"That was your goal. My goal is to do more."

"Sometimes doing more can put you on your ass, then what?"

Rachel left her mother's house disappointed and second guessing her decision to accept the money. Maybe keeping the business at home is the safest route for right now.

....

Rachel has successfully allowed a few negative people to make her second guess her craft, her ability to be fruitful, and distorted her usual positive outlook on life. This opportunity is what she has been working for her entire life, yet it is being shadowed by the doubt created in others.

This happens so much that it may be hard to identify. Mostly, it's going to come from the five closest people in your life. You probably could care less about the other people, you'll just call them haters anyway. No matter how positive you are, no matter how much Oprah you watch, if you are constantly engaging in negative relationships, conversations, and thoughts...there is no way for you to be positive. Imagine living with someone who is always negative. When do you get the chance to be positive? His/her negativity will snuff your little vibes out so fast it'll make your head spin. Energy and vibrations are a thing. I challenge you to do some self-study on the two. I have energy, you have energy, and the people you hang around have energy. Have you ever been somewhere and then someone who is super negative all the time walk in the room and totally throw off the energy? You may even say, "*Uh, his presence just ruined my mood!*" It's the energy that he's giving off. Energy is not verbal, it's spiritual.

The key to all of this is determining who your positive clique is and accepting who's in the negative clique. That doesn't mean that I have 86th these people from my life. It simply means that I do not ask these people for advice, I do not share ideas/hopes with them, and I do not include them on things that require good vibes. We have all heard, keep the vibe killers out of our circles, but sometimes that means eliminating parents and people we have known our whole lives. That's not reasonable, but it is reasonable to limit your contact and dealings with these people. I know negative people and some I love dearly. I don't have to erase their existence, I just have to know they are negative and know our relationships are limited due to their negativity.

In time they may see the light and decide to change on their own, but in the meantime you are tested with the feat of maintaining some sort of relationship without allowing it to affect your energy. These are the people you deal with "with a ten foot pole" as they say. As for your true circle, make sure their energy is similar to yours. You should feed off of each other. If you are the only light in a dark room, I suggest you find another room.

Chapter 4

If you have one smile in you, give it to the people you love. Don't surly at home, then go out in the street and start grinning 'Good Morning' at total strangers."

If you have one smile in you, give it to the people you love. Don't surly at home, then go out in the street and start grinning 'Good Morning' at total strangers."

~Dr. Maya Angelou

Have you ever met someone who seemed to suffer from multiple-personalities disorder? While that is a *very real* diagnosis, I'm speaking of someone who does not suffer from the *very real* disorder, but who is one way around strangers, yet totally different around people they have a personal relationship with. Have you ever shared space with someone who is a bouncing ball of cheerfulness to the world, but boorish and sullen in their own intimate dwellings?

Fake. Bogus. Phony. Do these words come to mind when thinking of such a person? If you are a woman who finds life in the presence of unfamiliar people, does that make you a fake person because you can't seem to find that light in the ones you are supposed to love? At times, our living situations aren't ideal. Maybe we are sharing our space with a bunch of unruly, ungrateful teenagers. Maybe we are sharing our space with a significant other after the spark has long disappeared. Maybe we are sharing our space with a roommate who is messy and completely unaware of boundaries. Whatever the case may be, we are left to share energies with someone who doesn't ignite warmth in our souls. We find ourselves saving that for our other life, the one we display to the world; not the one we hide.

This is 30

Joanne is in her late thirties, and after being a career chick for sixteen years, she decided to tackle the role of stay-at-home-mom. Her husband? She doesn't have one. Her boyfriend? It's complicated. Actually, it's not that complicated at all. Despite Joanne and her beau becoming parents over a year ago, they are still playing the high school courtship game. A high school courtship is when the couple does not live together, but there are frequent, random acts of sexual activity that involves little to no authentic emotion. There is also a lot of drama, I mean a lot of drama. On any occasion, you can find Joanne performing a drive-by to see who's occupying his attention, or calling/texting his phone with obscene threats because he hasn't seen the baby in over a week or so. When she first met Jason, they were so in-love. They went everywhere together. She knew he was a ladies man, but she thought that he would change after she got pregnant. Her career didn't correspond well with motherhood. After attempting to go back to work, finding a reliable baby-sitter, nursing the baby, and meeting deadlines…working just didn't seem like the best thing to do until the baby was older. It's not a decision she easily made, it's a decision she thought would be best for her and her son.

No matter how much fun parenthood was supposed to be, Joanne just doesn't understand the hype of it all. She loves her little baby, and she's equally happy that he's just as healthy as could be…but she doesn't find the joy that everybody said would be waiting for her after he was born. Most of her day is spent catering to his every need. When he cries, she must jump up. When he falls, she must jump up. When he soils his diaper, she must jump up. When he's hungry, she must jump up. When he's sick, she must jump up. Hell when he's happy, she must jump up.

She doesn't get much sleep because he doesn't sleep well, and when he is sleep, she is left to complete a thousand chores and find time for herself. Sure things would be easier if she had a mate who actually took his responsibilities of fatherhood seriously, but he doesn't and she's left feeling desperate and unfulfilled.

Sadly, the only outlet Joanne has is when she is away from Jason and her baby. There are times when she goes out with her friends and instantly feel a spark of life. There are times when she visits the supermarket and just allow herself to indulge in being separated from the things/people that cause her sadness. From the outside looking in, she's still a beautiful woman and new mom. But on the inside, she's lonely, unhappy, bitter and resentful. Pictures posted of her family show someone who is comfortable in her new role, loving life, loving the freedom of not having to clock in to a job every day. Ironically, people who do not know Joanne think that she has the ideal life. She made wise financial decisions at an early age; therefore, money isn't a problem for her. Not to mention that her son's father is pretty financially supportive, he just sucks at being a father and a partner.

There are some people in Joanne's life that know the two people she portray. They find it funny that she posts all these pictures of her kissing and loving on her son, when she barely notices him when they are alone. During the day, he mostly sits in his playpen crying for attention. At one point, her sisters wanted to stage an intervention for what they considered depression, but then they see her when she's not around family, and she's very happy. She's not the grouchy, overbearing, insensitive person that they know. They concluded that maybe family doesn't make you friends. Maybe she just has some unresolved issues with them. So they left her alone, and they distanced themselves.

Obviously Joanne suffers from a lot of things. She very well could be suffering from Post-Partum Depression, but more than anything, she suffers from bad decisions. Getting involved with a guy who wasn't on the same emotional level that she was on is problem number one. Agreeing to, or even planning to start a family based on what she thought would evoke change in her partner is problem number two. Problem number three is knowing that something is off with you mentally and emotionally and instead of dealing with it head-on, you search for outlets that in my opinion, only prolongs and intensifies the problem.

Although this book is not intended for just thirty year olds, in Joanne's case, she is knocking on forty and should be in a different head space than your average twenty year old. In many instances age does not identify how immature or mature one may be, or how wise or foolish they are. However, *This is 30* is intended to highlight areas in all of our lives that call for growth at certain points in development. At this stage in life, Joanna should not find it acceptable to waste her time chasing a man who has proven that he is not ready for the type of relationship that she wants, or the responsibility of being a father. In fact, Joanne doesn't seem to qualify for the "Mother of the Year" award herself.

Some of you may be thinking, her being a neglectful mother is the worst thing Joanne has going for her. While others of you may be thinking that Joanne not knowing who she is, and not being connected to those things that make her illuminate will ultimately lead to her downfall. Which is the truer statement?

I can imagine that being a mother is a tiresome, all-consuming job. It's a job that does not come with instructions or a "How-To" manual. It is something that is felt and learned as time progresses. As a woman, besides being a mother, when you remove yourself from *feeling*, you simply become a shell of a person. Being without feeling is being numb, there's no ifs, ands or buts about that. Try putting an ice cube on your skin for an hour.

In the event that you find yourself feeling numb around anyone that you share your energy with, it's time to take ownership of your life and make some serious changes. Finding those happy outlets in others only deceives your brain into thinking that everything is OK, when it's not. Those are the women who become complacent with unhappiness. Those are the women who rest in resentfulness. Those are the women who bath in bitterness. Because guess what? In your mind, you're thinking…"if I can only get to 3:00". Or whatever time your outlet happens. It then becomes a viscous cycle. In this scenario, Joanne saves her smiles and happiness for events/places that do not require her to be a mother or a woman who is in a relationship with a cheater. I do not think that Joanne has a problem with her sisters, but they know her secret; her unhappiness. It then becomes necessary to exclude these people from her life because being around them is just another reminder of the grief although they are not directly the cause of it.

If you ever find yourself escaping, remember that there is no way for you to be who you were uniquely designed to be when you are constantly dodging the barrier that stands between you and bliss. Of course it's not easy, if that were the case everybody would be running around singing jingles, snapping fingers, and dancing through life. Depending on your situation, it can be hard. It may take more courage than you think you have. If nothing else, remember the euphoric feeling that comes with the escape. Don't you deserve to be that person every day? Don't you deserve that peace? Here's to smiling…all the damn time.

Chapter 5

"I, with a deeper instinct choose a man who compels my strength, who makes enormous demands on me, who does not doubt my courage or my toughness, who does not believe me naïve or innocent, who has the courage to treat me like a woman."

> **"I, with a deeper instinct choose a man who compels my strength, who makes enormous demands on me, who does not doubt my courage or my toughness, who does not believe me naïve or innocent, who has the courage to treat me like a woman."**
>
> **~Anais Nin**

Irene stands before the crowd of anxious, energetic women. They are screaming and cheering as she swallows enough breath to blow out the thirty-one candles on her birthday cake. To everyone else, Irene is living the dream. She has a loving, faithful, fine-as-wine husband, a huge house, the latest luxury car, and all the designer shoes her massive closet can hold. There is not one single thing on the planet that Irene could ask for that she can't have…as it relates to material things. In today's society, that seems to be the measuring stick for happiness and success.

Irene closes her eyes and drifts back to her life just three years ago. She had a pretty decent career, selling real estate in Atlanta's premier neighborhoods. She had a solid group of friends that she spent her free time with. She had healthy relationships with most of the people in her family. She was happy, and she was doing the damn thing. Sure her love life was a bit inconsistent, but that was by design. Irene got a kick out of being a mass dater in Atlanta. With the down-low brothers, the serial cheaters, and the married men searching for a little side candy…she just didn't have time to be bothered with trying to establish anything worthwhile. It has been said that the ratio is one hundred men to five women. That might be a bit exaggerated, but Atlanta is a pretty difficult place to find a genuine relationship. From Irene's perspective, every one she met had an agenda.

She met John through a mutual friend. It was supposed to be a fun fling, nothing lasting. He had a shit load of money and he needed a new house. The way Irene saw it, she could get a couple of handbags out of him, and the fat commission that came with the kind of house he was searching for. He was charming, but not in a pseudo, sleazy way. He just had a way about him that was different than the other ballers she had dated. He didn't talk about his money all of the time, and he wouldn't buy her a handbag, no matter how low-cut her dress was, or how much she overly flirted with him. He wanted to talk about stocks and bonds and current events. He wasn't the least bit impressed with her Porsche or her red bottoms. He didn't invite her to high profile events, they didn't even go out on the town that often. He would rent out secluded places so they could *"get to know each other"*. Irene found herself letting her guard down and returning to her Alabama roots. The person she was before the city life. The person she was before she allowed society to deem who she was supposed to be.

The rest is history. They dated. He courted her at the level of greatness that would make her deceased father proud. He let it be known that he had relationship goals and he wasn't interested in playing games. She found herself becoming exclusive with John, and then he proposed. It was a little sudden, and Irene was a little taken aback. She knew exactly who he was and what he wanted from life, but they had not spent a large amount of time talking about her goals and dreams. She shared her concerns with her close friends and family members. They quieted the doubts that were circling around in her head. They assured her that John was a stand-up guy and she'd be a fool to let him slip through her fingertips all because they hadn't gotten around to a few career conversations.

Irene believed them. She convinced herself that everything would be okay. And it was, for about two years. John was the perfect man. But then things changed. The more Irene would try to corner him about going back to work, or finishing her degree, the angrier he became with her. He wasn't an abusive man. His anger came in different forms. He would have her cook a seven-course meal, and then skip out at the last minute. Or he would excitedly talk about an event for weeks, and then tell Irene at the last hour that he didn't think she should accompany him. His get back was passive aggressive in nature, and always resulted in her sitting in their mansion alone while he was out enjoying life. When she brought these things to his attention he would pretend that he didn't know what she was talking about, and that career, academic driven women wouldn't have time to do those types of things anyway.

Irene became resentful. She resented him as a man, and she resented their marriage. She felt like a well-dressed prisoner. She started to notice that John orchestrated every aspect of their life. She was rewarded when she went with the flow, and punished when she went against the grain. But Irene comes from a stock of strong women, and she wasn't going out without a fight. When John was away for business, she began to use her time wisely. She renewed her real estate license, and started researching online degrees. Maybe John was worried about her being away from home a lot. Maybe if she showed him that she could do everything she wanted to do without being gone all the time, just maybe he would support her.

Irene successfully enrolled in an online graduate program. She hired a personal assistant and assigned her the task of combing Atlanta's housing market for the most expensive, luxurious homes out there. She hired a professional graphic designer, web designer, and videographer to create a website that showcased pictures of each home, with a custom interactive tour. Irene and her team met virtually every week, establishing a strong marketing presence online, even coining herself as the "go to" for luxury homes in Atlanta. It took about six months to put everything together. She wanted her business plan to be flawless when she presented it to John. She was hoping that at the very least he would offer her emotional support. She still needed a financial backer for some innovative ideas she wanted to implement on her website, but she knew she couldn't count on John to support her in that way.

The morning of her thirty-first birthday, Irene presented everything to John in a silvery wrapped package. Inside the package was a print out of her first semester grades (all A's) and an Ipad that displayed her website. She even included a portfolio of all of her marketing materials. It took John a minute to understand what he was looking at. He quickly flipped through the web pages, thumbed through a few brochures, briefly scanned the transcript, and then placed everything back into the package. Irene waited like a kid on Christmas for a "job well done" or "I'm so proud of you baby".

It never came. He told her that he couldn't believe she went behind his back. He told her that he wasn't interested in dating a woman with male ambition. He said he thought that she was comfortable with the life he provided her. He said that it was an insult to his manhood that his wife is still searching for more, even after getting more than she ever had. He told her that the graduate degree would not make her more money than she was making with an undergraduate degree, and that the housing market was changing. He said it's not smart to start a business in a market that will soon crash.

Irene looked at all of her hard work through blurred vision. She heard him talking but his words didn't quite register. Certain words rung in her ears, but the majority of his conversation was met with deaf ears. She was already prepared for this moment. Although she was banking on a positive outcome, she knew that she had to expect the worse. That's why she had already picked out a new place to lease, and had scheduled a professional mover. You know, just in case shit went left.

"*Girl, is this a party or what?*" She snaps out of her thoughts to face her mother, who is motioning for her to blow out the candles.

Irene picks up the microphone, and nervously brings it to her lips. "*I want to say something before I blow out my candles.*"

The room is instantly hushed.

"I want to say that the past year has been the most rewarding year of my life. I have cried myself to sleep more than you would ever imagine. I have pushed myself in ways I never thought I could. I have used every penny I have on a hope and a dream. I've basically reinvented myself. This new journey requires change. It requires more from me than I have been willing to give to myself in the past. It requires for me to be better to myself, and it also requires for me to only allow people in my circle who are interested in treating me at the standard that I am treating myself. Certain people didn't make the cut. Yeah I know some of you are whispering about who's here and who's not here. Well he's not coming. He's not running late. This year, I decided it was more important to be myself instead of someone's trophy wife. I decided that a union is not when one person dictates the life of another. I decided that if my dreams were not accepted and respected, then there was no point in a union at all. That's a dictatorship, not a partnership. This year, I decided to be free. Will I stumble? Of course. Will I fail? Absolutely. But I'm ready for everything that comes with the freedom to be myself. I was dreading this birthday for so long because I couldn't imagine where I would be or what I would be doing. Well it's here and I'm better than ever. Every heartache and disappointment has brought me to this very place. This statement is not a proclamation of the dissolution of my marriage, but a statement of hope and courage. As you celebrate me tonight, celebrate something real. Celebrate my fierceness, celebrate my bravery, and celebrate my journey."

Irene passes the microphone to her mother who is standing there with a pool of tears in her eyes. She expected people to be silent. She expected them to be neutral. But that's not what happened. She turned around and there was a line of eager friends waiting to celebrate her, the real Irene.

....

Irene learned a very important lesson that a lot of us learn the hard way. Irene noticed the red flags, but instead of slowing down and exercising patience, she listened to other people and ignored all the signs. Some of you may be thinking, well he didn't seem like a bad guy. He wasn't a bad guy; he just wasn't right guy for Irene. If he had married a woman who was okay with being a stay-at-home wife, I'm sure they would still be married today. If Irene had found a man who valued her professional career, she would still be married today.

Although as women we share many similarities, we are all different and unique in our own way. We have to find someone who brings out our uniqueness. We have to find someone who brings out the best in us. We have to find someone who wants us to have a voice. You know what kind of woman you are. You know what kind of woman you want to be. Be with someone who accepts you. Be with someone who respects you. Be with someone who embraces you. Be with someone who supports you. Be with someone who compliments you. And most importantly, be with someone who isn't afraid to treat you like the woman you are, and the woman you want to be.

Chapter 6

"Nobody can hurt me without my permission."

"Nobody can hurt me without my permission."
-Mahatma Gandhi

It has been said that heartache and heartbreak are the worst kinds of pain known to mankind. Heartache and heartbreak can come in many different forms. It can be from a lover, a family member, a friend, the lost of a loved one, or a slew of frequent, soul-crushing disappointments. When we are in the midst of the storm, it can seem as if we have absolutely no control over what's happening to us. In the midst of the storm, our eyes cannot stop crying, our chest cannot stop heaving, our lips won't smile, and our happiness seems so very far away. We often find ourselves questioning every person, and every aspect of our lives.

"Why is he treating me this way?"

"Why did she betray me?"

"Why would she use me like that?"

"Why can't he see my worth?"

We're asking every question, but the right question. The right question is, "why am I allowing myself to be mistreated by others?" That's the only question that truly deserves an answer and reflection, because those other questions are still based on the responses of the people who are causing you to feel a certain way. Those questions are still putting the power in someone else's reach. You have the power. You are the only person responsible for how you treat yourself. Sure, we would love for the people we meet to treat us with the utmost respect and loyalty, but life isn't fair and we can't write out the script for the actions of other people.

....

The sound of holiday cheer is ringing from every corner of the mall. Jackie is busy finishing up her last face for the day. She was left to pick up a part-time gig at Estee Lauder after Darnell left her high and dry a few weeks ago. Jackie and Darnell have been on-and-off for about four years. He's the only man that she's ever really loved. He's also the only man that has the power to make her day better or make her day a living hell. Three weeks ago, Darnell moved out of their apartment after Jackie read some text messages he had been sending to one of his ex girlfriends. Darnell had gone to the dentist earlier that day to get two wisdom teeth extracted. Jackie had loved on him and took care of his every need for the entire day. After his last dose of hydrocodone for the night, Jackie decided to go through Darnell's phone to see if he had really changed. She just needed confirmation that he wasn't up to his old tricks, and that he was more focused on them building a solid life together. They had recently gone ring shopping and Jackie just needed to know that she wasn't making a mistake by forgiving all of his past indiscretions. Of course every thing in her told her not to do it, but she threw caution to the wind, and punched in his six-digit passcode anyway.

Jackie's heart dropped and the pit of her stomach roared from sadness as she thumbed through Darnell's iMessages and read his conversations with his ex girlfriend. Not only were they still seeing each other, Darnell had promised her that he was going to leave Jackie just as soon as he received his tax refund check at the beginning of the year. He assured her that the money would be used to pay down on a new apartment. He told her that he still loved her. He told her that he enjoyed being with her last night. He told her that he would never love Jackie the way he loved her. He told her that what he and Jackie shared was just temporary. He told her that Jackie was annoying and desperate and that he wouldn't ever marry or have children with such an insecure woman.

With tears streaming down her face, Jackie placed the phone back where she found it. With everything in her, she wished she had never looked. She wished she could erase every word that was now imprinted her on her heart. She paced the floor for about two hours trying to figure out what she had done wrong to make this man treat her so badly. She tried to make sense of the betrayal, but she couldn't. She packed an overnight bag and left Darnell a letter to tell him what she saw. The next day, she expected him to call and plead with her, but he didn't. She came home to an empty house.

Jackie's been in a funk since that day. She tried to call Darnell, but he sends her to voicemail. She tried to text him, but he won't respond. She wanted to apologize for going through his phone, and she also wanted an explanation for his actions. Apparently he didn't feel that she deserved an explanation. Every attempt has gone unanswered. Christmas is drawing near, but Jackie is definitely not in the spirit. Watching couples aimlessly float through the mall, holding hands and sniffing perfumes makes her skin crawl. She wasn't the perfect girlfriend, and they both had areas that they needed to work on, but for the life of her, she just can't understand why a man would go through so much trouble to deceive someone when he could just be single.

"Hey Jack! Are you going to visit your parents for the holidays?" Bonnie places a basket of sample lipstick tubes under the counter.

Jackie rolls her eyes while carefully applying bronzer to her client's face. "Oh no. The last thing I need right now is to be around a bunch of holly jolly people. Girl I think I'm just going to be a Grinch and stay at home this year."

Bonnie pouts her lower lip and gives Jackie a concerned look. "Aw Jack, I think it'll do you good to be around people. Being alone on Christmas can suck big time! Believe me, I've been there and done that."

Jackie continues to brush colorful, shimmering powder on the lady's eyes. "I have a question for you. How did you bounce back after Malcolm cheated on you last year? How did you get over it?"

"It was hard. I'm still not *over it*. I miss the good times. I felt the exact same way you feel right now. Malcolm wasn't going to change. Every year it was a different woman. Just when I thought we were on good terms, he'd do something else. It was a never-ending cycle of abuse."

"So what was the final straw? What did he do to make you finally leave?"

Bonnie flips her blonde hair out of her eyes. She smiles wickedly and shakes her head in amusement. "Actually, the day I left him he didn't do anything major. I mean, he was texting on his phone and being secretive, but it wasn't anything he hadn't done a thousand times before. I simply just decided to stop putting myself on the receiving end of his crap. I was tired of bargaining with him to treat me right."

Jackie rolls her eyes and smacks her lips. "Okay Dr. Phil, I thought you were going to give me some real advice. Here you are quoting Iyanla quotes."

Bonnie laughs. "Seriously Jackie, I just really started to think about my situation. I had been with this man for six years. He had cheated on me for *all* six years. Every time he cheated, I took him back. Every time he cheated, I told myself that I could fix him and that I could be better so that he would be better towards me. When I was happy, it was because he did something to make me happy. When I was sad, it was because he did something to make me sad. It was just so tiring! I wanted off of that merry-go-round."

The older lady that Jackie is working on slightly shakes her head without causing a sudden movement. "Lord, don't I remember those days. Chile, I wouldn't pay to be young and dumb again."

This is 30

Jackie laughs at her client. "Mrs. Nancy, you can relate? I thought you and Mr. Joe were always happy."

"We are happy. I wasn't always with Joe. I had my fair share of scumbags. But to be fair, I was more of the problem to myself than they were. You see, can't no man treat you bad if you don't allow him to treat you that way. There will be times when you are hurt, that's all apart of the relationship game, but you don't have to be a spectator to your own hurt. You can stop it at any moment. You can decide that you deserve more. You can pick better men. You can stop putting all your happiness in one person. You can be your own damn lover. Ya'll young girls better get wise before you find yourself used up and miserable, missing out on life because you've played victim and deemed yourself powerless."

Tears fill Jackie's eyes and she quickly dabs at the corners. "It's easier said than done."

"So are a lot of things, but does that mean you don't try? I'm sure Cosmetology school wasn't a walk in the park, but you decided that you wanted to be successful, so you stuck on in there. Same thing. You can decide you want to be happy and work towards being happy."

"I guess you're right. Men just make things so damn hard!"

Mrs. Nancy grabs a hand mirror and examines her newly stained lips. "No baby, you're making it hard on yourself. Stop giving people permission to hurt you."

Instead of Jackie acknowledging the actions of her lover and holding him accountable for how he was treating her, she immediately began to internalize his actions and blame herself. Obviously Darnell had moved on to someone else, but Jackie continued to reach out to him and apologize for her actions. Don't get me wrong; I don't think that she should have looked through his phone. This can be a big debate topic among women. Some women think it's perfectly fine to take a peep every now and again.

I would disagree. If you have a man who has given you access to his phone, that's one thing. If you're looking and he does not know it, you're being deceptive and untrustworthy.

I use to hear older women say, "I sure wish I knew then what I know now." At the time, it just seemed like a way to get their point across. As I grow older, I acquire more wisdom. As you grow older, you acquire more wisdom. Our biggest assignment is to use those mistakes and growing pains as tools for success for our *right now*. It's time for us to take ownership and accountability of our lives, our happiness, and our shortcomings. It's time for us to give people permission to treat us the way we want to be treated, and walk away from those who refuse to.

Chapter 7

Stay close to the wild ones, for those are the ones that will inspire you."

"Stay close to the wild ones, for those are the ones that will inspire you."
-Unknown

Traditionally, I think most of us were taught to play it safe. I'm not sure if our parents knew that's what they were instilling in us, but it definitely was the overall message as we grew from baby to toddler, to toddler to child, to child to teenager, and from teenager to adult. Just think about that for a minute. When we were babies and toddlers, we couldn't roam to far away from an adult, there was no need to explore. We even began to develop our limited taste buds because of our parents' inability to stray away from the norm. There was no way that our parents were going to spend extra money on a different jar of Gerber when they knew exactly what jar of food we already liked.

Little by little we were taught the art of routine, and the art of playing it safe. Even as teenagers, people told us what we did well, our grades reflected what our favorite subject in school was supposed to be...so we went with it. Meaning, if we received a consistent "A" in Biology, we definitely were expected to go to Medical or Nursing school. If we consistently received good grades in History, we were definitely expected to be the next great attorney. We coined our hopes and dreams from what our parents wanted us to be. We went to the colleges they wanted us to attend. We wore the clothes they picked out, or the clothes everybody else thought were cool. Rarely did we ever break out of the shell to go left when everyone else was going right. There was no need to. We literally had someone to think about our every move, and make our every decision.

Now think about the crazy girl from high school. You know, the one who adorned blue hair to prom, the one who wore distressed jeans before they became a thing, the one who raised her hand even when the teacher had explained the problem, all because she didn't agree with the answer. She is the girl who wrote "F*ck college!" in the "Future Goals" section of the yearbook. She's the girl who had a different boyfriend every week, simply because they couldn't keep her attention. She's the girl that *never* did what was expected of her. She's a wild one.

....

It's a breezy April day. The sun has yet to cast its' rays on the earth. The daffodils are in full bloom, spreading springtime cheer to walkers and runners as they pound the pavement. Friendship Park is the daily meeting spot for Carmen and Amanda. They are both art teachers at the area high school. After a long day of battling teenagers, there's nothing that the two women desire more than sweating out their frustrations on the walking trial.

They've been friends ever since they entered the doors of Eastside High School. They were two young girls, straight out of college, clueless on what it meant to be an adult. Throughout the years, they leaned on each other. Although they are totally different in every way, they both share a love for visually beautiful things, and a love for teaching. Amanda is the outspoken one. She's the one who will debate their administrator on the art supply budget until she gets what she wants. Carmen is the shy one. She's always somewhere in the background, observing, taking notes, and quietly going about her life.

Amanda stoops down to tie her sneakers, while shoving her car keys in her fannie pack. "How was school today?"

Carmen lunges forward and sideways, stretching her legs. "It was just an ordinary day, nothing exciting happened. We did have a fight on our hall, but that's about it."

Amanda folds her arms and looks her friend dead in the eyes. "So you're not going to ask me why I called out? When did you stop being so nosey?"

Carmen laughs a little before taking a swig of lemon flavored Dasani. "I know why you were out. You were probably out on this new studio manhunt."

Amanda smiles. "Carmen, I'm just so excited! You really should reconsider doing this with me. I actually signed on a place today. My search is officially over. No more waking up and dreading the day. No more watching the clock. No more feeling like my purpose isn't being fulfilled."

Worry spreads across Carmen's forehead, causing her eyes to squint and her skin to crinkle. "Just like that? You haven't even been approved for the bank loan yet. Was that a good idea Amanda? How will you make the lease payment if your loan is denied?"

"Thanks for the congratulations. I'm sooooo happy that I have a friend like you." Amanda's voice is laced with sarcasm.

"Hey, that's not fair. I'm just playing devils advocate. I'm just looking out for you."

"Are you looking out for me, or are you hating because you're too scared to do this with me?"

Carmen's pale face turns three shades of red. "Are you serious? Hater? I've never been a hater. I told you from the start that I wasn't quitting my job. I can't believe you're throwing this in my face!"

"I'm not throwing anything in your face, I'm simply reminding you that there's more to life than us clocking in to a job we both hate, being unappreciated, and living paycheck-to-paycheck."

Carmen starts power walking, cocking her head back when she speaks. "Speak for yourself. I don't hate what I do."

Amanda gasps. "Yes you do! We both do! We've talked about it a million times! We both would rather deal with adults who appreciate the art, opposed to dealing with a bunch of ungrateful brats who could care less about being enrolled in a meaningless elective. "

"I'm not quitting my job. I have children. I have a mortgage. It's just too risky."

"Carmen, think about it. I found this cool spot that has the most modern furniture, I'm thinking stark white so that the contrast will be…"

Carmen stops and angrily faces Amanda. "I'm not quitting my job. I can't believe you're trying to force your wild ideas on me. That's your personality, that's not mine. Don't criticize me because I'm not careless. It's 100% careless to quit a good paying job and bank on grown people to pay you to paint flowers and puppies!"

Amanda takes in the scenery. She stares at her friend of nineteen years. Part of her is angry with Carmen for insulting her. The bigger part of her is sad because her friend would rather play it safe and report to a job she no longer finds enjoyable than answering the call on her life. "Wow. Careless? Carmen, you are the most talented artist I've ever met. I've always told you that. I wanted you to do this with me because I know that we can be successful. Of course I'm afraid. Of course I've second-guessed myself a million times, but today I took a leap. I'm doing this with or without you. I guess you're right. It is my personality. I've never been the kind of person to walk on the grass to let other people walk by. I've always felt that I deserved to walk on the sidewalk too."

Carmen let out a big sigh. "Maybe we shouldn't workout today. I'm no longer in the mood. Maybe we will get together another day. I'm happy that you're doing what you want to do, I just wish you'd respect the fact that it's not something I want to do."

Another day doesn't happen for some time. Amanda goes on to open a highly successful Sip and Paint, and Carmen continues to teach 9th grade Art Appreciation. A minor disagreement caused a major divide in their friendship that day. While Amanda respects Carmen's position, it was clear that her friend resents her out-of-the-box, risk-taking personality. Days turned into months, and months turned into a whole year. Amanda's studio becomes so successful; she is forced to open a larger studio, which means more people and longer hours.

Amanda decides to pay her old friend a visit at Friendship Park one sunny afternoon.

"Hey girly." It's clear Amanda isn't there to exercise. She's fully dressed in jeans and loafers.

Carmen is a little stunned, but more embarrassed that she allowed so much time to go by without apologizing for her actions that day. "Amanda. Hi, how are you?"

In true Amanda fashion, she reaches out and plucks at Carmen's brown yoga top. "Where did you find this thing? Can we get some color in your wardrobe?"

Carmen laughs. Not because the joke is that funny. She laughs to keep from crying. "I see you haven't changed one bit! I think my top is nice."

"It's ugly. Very ugly." She reaches for a hug and is instantly overwhelmed with emotion when Carmen returns the embrace.

"I missed you so much Amanda. I'm so sorry for how I acted that day. You were right; I should have listened to you and trusted your vision. I wasn't' happy at work, I was just so fearful. You can be a little wild with your thoughts sometimes and I just didn't want to follow you down a hole I couldn't dig myself out of. You acted like quitting our jobs and following our dreams was as easy as slicing pie. That scared me."

"I know. And I should have been more understanding. Our differences are what made us strong. I never meant for my excitement to turn into aggression. I was always taught to jump and build my parachute on the way down."

"Congratulations on everything. You're doing so well! I read about your place all the time."

"That's kind of why I'm here." Amanda pulls out a pair of keys.

Carmen wrinkles her brows in confusion. "I don't understand."

"You're the most talented artist I know. I'm opening a new, bigger studio. I need you. Trust me. For once, be wild, be careless, don't play it safe."

The familiar feeling of fear tugged in Carmen's throat, but this time she swallowed it back down. "I'm ready now. Thank you for inspiring me to see what I couldn't envision on my own."

....

How many wild ones have you met over your thirty-something years? Aren't they the ones who seem to hear a rhythm of music that you cannot hear? Aren't they the ones who seem to *always* land on their feet? Aren't they the ones that you wish you could be…even for just one hour? These women are appealing because of their ability to see the glass as half full. They are not afraid of failure. More importantly, they are not afraid of living.

Sometimes, we have to gravitate to the wild ones, especially if you are the type to follow all of the rules and never take the path less traveled. Being wild does not always mean being wreckless and irresponsible. Sometimes, being wild simply means having courage. Sometimes, being wild simply means having the audacity to think that you deserve a life worth living. Here's to the wild ones. May you continue to inspire people with your bravery and ability to see the world as one big adventure.

Chapter 8

"No matter how big or soft or warm your bed is, you have to get out of it."

"No matter how big or soft or warm your bed is, you have to get out of it."

-Grace Slick

There are some women who are natural-born go-getters. Finding their niche in their professional world comes easy to them. They are super focused on their goals, and they will not accept nothing less than what they envision for their lives. We know women who are like this. We aspire to be a woman like this. Hell, some of us are the women I'm speaking of. The perception is, these women have the world at their feet. The perception is, these women do not have to work very hard; they climb the career ladder effortlessly. The perception is, they are an overnight success.

Those perceptions can't be further from the truth. The reality is, they work very hard. The reality is, they are up making things happen while most of us are sound asleep. The reality is, nothing was given to them. The reality is, they've stumbled more times than we can count, but they understand that failure is just a stepping stone to success. We watch these women with green-eyed envy. We tell ourselves that once we get that "big break" that we will be just like them. The only problem is, some of us lack their work ethic. Some of us lack their drive, some of us let a few stumbling blocks stop us in our tracks, and some of us are just lazy as hell.

Opportunity has never been as close to us as it is today. We can literally be anything that we want to be. We can literally go anywhere that we want to go. Traditionally, women have made excellent homemakers, raising children and catering to their husbands. Today, women are running multi-million dollar companies, and creating innovative start-ups. No matter what career path you would like to embark upon, there is a wealth of information at your fingertips to map out how to get there. You just have to wake up in the morning, get out of your bed, and get to work.

....

Claudine is in her mid-thirties, recently divorced, with three small children at home. Claudine and her husband, Hank, were married for ten years before deciding to go their separate ways. When they were younger, Hank enjoyed having his wife at home waiting for him after a long, stressful day at the office. Claudine would have dinner cooked and the house cleaned. On most nights, he could even count on her to have on a sexy little number. After he finished law school and started his own firm, the money started pouring in. They were financially doing better than most of the people they knew. Claudine started to nag Hank about having children. She said that having children would make their lives complete. She said that she needed something to do during the day.

Hank is eight years older than Claudine, so he's been around the block more times than she has. He wasn't overly excited about Claudine having children without having a career. He grew up in a household that resembled the life Claudine was so desperate to recreate. Hank's mother was a stay-at-home mom. She was great at it too. There was never a time when they didn't have a home cooked meal, or freshly ironed clothes, or perfectly made beds. His father did the working, and his mother did the loving. But he saw how lonely and incomplete his mother became the older they got. She was often very overbearing and very over-protective. Hank also watched his mother and his father fall out of love. Her life was centered on her kids, and when they left to start their own lives, there was nothing left for her to do.

Hank did not want this for Claudine. When he fell in love with her, she was an aspiring journalist, with enough energy to fill an empty room. She was beautiful and happy and excited about her life. After they got married, she settled into the wife role, and became obsessed with catering to his every need. After a few failed attempts at journalism, she started to resent the field and began to focus all of her energy on having children. It's like the children were going to fill a void that her career could not fill. She became less focused on her career, and more focused on having babies.

Eventually, Hank gave in and agreed to start trying for a family. Five months later, they found out they were having twins. Claudine was the happiest he had ever seen her, and he just didn't have the heart to communicate his concerns to her. Months turned into years, and soon they had three busy little boys running around their home. Hank was busier than ever at the firm, and Claudine was occupied with being a mom. She stopped cooking hearty meals, and opted for quick fixes. She stopped doing the laundry everyday, and opted to wash a few loads one day a week. She stopped getting her hair fixed. She stopped wearing sexy little numbers. She stopped noticing when he came in and when he left. They became roommates.

After two years, Hank asked for a divorce. Claudine never had time to see the therapist he hired, she never seemed interested in working things out, so he just gave up. Now, Claudine finds herself taking care of two six year olds, and a four year old all by herself. Hank was ordered to pay alimony and child support, which will cover the expenses for the household. Although it seems as if Claudine has it made, she goes to sleep in a fist full of tears every night. Not because she misses her husband, but because she misses who she used to be. She misses who she wanted to be at this point in her life. She thought thirty-five would look different for her.

Because the twins are school age, she finds herself glued to Facebook and Instagram during the day, living vicariously through the lives of strangers. She's following a hand full of people she went to college with, and she can't believe how successful some of them have become. It's like they kept living, but her life stopped. Every day she tells herself that she's going to draft up a resume, schedule to get some professional photos taken, and try to get back in the game. But every day, she finds herself thumbing through countless profiles, drawn into their world, and carelessly passing the day by.

Soon, nine o'clock in the morning turns into nine o'clock at night, and she hasn't accomplished anything.

Her friends think she's just lazy and have gotten accustomed to someone else taking care of her. On any given day, you can hear one of Claudine's loved ones whispering about how she's "fallen off" and how she's wasting all of her potential.

One night, Hank stops by the house to pick up the boys for a weekend of camping. Before he leaves, Claudine grabs him by the shoulder and stops him from walking out of the door.

"Hank. What happened to me?" Tears roll down her face in endless rows of sadness.

"I don't know Claudine. At first I thought it was the children, but I offered to get nannies and babysitters and whatever you needed to have a life outside of them. It's like you lost your will to be alive."

"To be alive? My God Hank, I'm not suicidal."

"That's not what I mean. I mean, you lost your will to get up and be ALIVE, you just started existing. You had your routines down packed, and you started finding ways to do things with the least amount of effort possible."

"You mean I became lazy?"

"Lazy. Withdrawn. Unfulfilled. You would say that you wanted to do all of these amazing things, but you never did them. Not even as it relates to your career, I'm talking about just everyday things. You would say you were going to make this grand dinner, and you never got around to it. You would say you were going to wash and fold all of the laundry, but you never got around to it. You would say that you're going to take an internship to get back into your profession, and you never did that. Hell, you said you were going to plant some flowers, I haven't seen one bud, one bloom, one petal."

Claudine smiled in spite of the heaviness of the conversation. "Once I realized that I wasn't going to get those journalism jobs I wanted, I started finding things to replace that, but those things didn't make me happy. To be honest, I thought I really wanted children, but it's very hard being a mom. I wouldn't have three if I could do it all over. I don't know, life just became disappointing and it seemed like it took more effort than I had to get things done."

Hank took Claudine by the hand. "I knew that would happen, that's why I pushed for you to find something you loved outside of us, your husband and your kids. Your life became about serving others, and you forgot about yourself. When people are unhappy, they are unmotivated."

Claudine thanked Hank for his honesty. She kissed her kids goodbye, and ran upstairs to find her old journals. She flipped through them page by page, in hopes of finding that spark that had long escaped her. She wouldn't find her motivation in one night, but she damn sure wasn't going to stop looking for it this time around.

....

Let me try to bring this home for some of you. A lot of women are lazy and withdrawn because they have carried disappointment, sadness, and failure around for far too long. Claudine used to be the go-getter I spoke so passionately about at the beginning of this chapter. In college, she was the woman that many envied. She was the woman that younger girls aspired to be. But do you see how failure can creep in like a thief in the night and turn you into someone totally different?

Because she didn't get those journalism jobs, she started trying to find success in other things. We still live in a society that celebrates marriage and babies more than they do a college graduation. I'm not trying to step on toes or say those things are not important, but if I've just received a degree in Chemical Engineering, why ya'll not throwing me a shower? Somebody should be singing. Somebody should be bringing me gifts.

Somebody should be hiring an event coordinator to help me celebrate. I'm just saying!

Claudine found that she couldn't fail at getting married and having children. She found success in those things, but eventually those things failed miserably. Why? Because they were temporary fillers for the things she really wanted. It's like having a brand new tire and then it goes on flat. You pull over and put on a spare tire. You ride that spare until it goes on flat, but you don't have another tire because that's the only temporary filler that you had for the original tire. You're going to be like Claudine, stuck on the side of the road with your thumb hanging out, waiting for the tow truck to come and help you.

It's a fine line between failure and success. It's a fine line between being the woman you want to be, and being the woman you settle for. Drive, motivation, consistency, purpose, and passion all play a major role in what side of the line you will be on. Don't let failure and disappointment stop you from waking up everyday with an urge to conquer the day. Drop that heavy load. You should wake up excited about your life every single day. I'm not saying you won't have bad days or bad situations to deal with, but when you are centered, there's an over-riding desire to throw that cover back, comb your hair, put on some clothes, look at yourself in the mirror, and win.

Chapter 9

"No person is your friend who demands your silence, or denies your right to grow."

"No person is your friend who demands your silence, or denies your right to grow."
-Alice Walker

Friendship. When we were younger, it was so easy to have and keep friends. The older I get, the less friends I have. Now that I'm in my thirties, it's all about quality. I could care less about having twenty friends if the quality of the friendship isn't there. People have started using the word "friend" too freely. Think about it, even Facebook refers to the people that follow you as "Friends". Those people aren't your friends! Because of the world we live you, it's not uncommon to hear, "Oh I don't know her like that, we're just Friends on Facebook." I get it; calling someone your "Friend" on Facebook was a way for them to brand themselves differently than other social media feeds. Instagram and Twitter refer to the people who follow you as "Followers", so I guess the use of the word "Friend" has a more welcoming connotation than the latter.

I said all that to say, using the word "friend" is something we just throw around. It doesn't have the same power as it once had. It doesn't have the same magic as it used to have. It doesn't have the same effect. More importantly, it doesn't have the same responsibilities as it used to have. Back in the day, my mama had the same friends. These women were apart of the fabric of my life. When I participated in pageants, they are the ones who helped my mama pick out my dresses. When my mama had to work late, they were the ones who made sure my brothers and I were able to attend the football games. When I tried out for class officer and homecoming maid, they were the ones rooting me on and helping me create cool election posters. When I had my first heartbreak, they were the ones wiping my tears away. For every moment in my life, whether good or bad, these women were there. I knew what friendships were supposed to look like based on these experiences.

Nowadays, friendships don't have the same lifespan as they once had. I can say that I am guilty of not having the same friends that I had in my twenties. To be clear, there are some friends that we have that we may not talk to everyday or every month. However, once we link back up it's like we were never apart. Those are life-long friends. In this chapter, I'm speaking about the friends that are apart of your day-to-day, the people you spend the most time with. The ones you tell your secrets to. The ones who know about every little detail of your life. Let's talk about the friends who cosign or fail to redirect your toxic behavior and lifestyle.

....

Tasha Lucas is fine. Not fine as in, she's doing well. Tasha has the perfect figure, 36-24-36. After being labeled as the "fat girl" throughout school, Tasha decided that she'd never fall victim to overeating and failing to take care of herself again. She has a new lifestyle and a new man. Tasha's been dating Michael for about a year. Things are heating up, and Michael is seriously thinking about proposing to Tasha. She's a hard worker, she's smart, she's funny, and she's humble. He's never met a woman quite like her. She has her moments of not being very confident, mostly because of her past weight insecurities, but overall she's the kind of woman you want to take off the market.

Tasha feels the exact same way as Michael does. She's gone through five boyfriends in the last two years. One guy was a serial cheater. One guy had a crazy baby mama who couldn't let go of the relationship. One guy had trust issues, he was jealous of the attention she got from other men. Another guy said he didn't ever want to be married, and the last guy just wasn't her type. She tried to make herself like him because she desperately wanted to be in a committed relationship, but he just wasn't the one. She met Michael through a mutual friend at the gym. They hit it off immediately. People were very surprised at how quickly the relationship developed. Tasha's friends were skeptical of Michael and his intentions. They felt like he was entirely too eager to get married. Something had to be wrong with him.

Tasha and Janet are workout buddies. They met at a fitness class three years ago, and have been friends since that moment. Janet is Tasha's ride or die. In the three years that they have been friends, they've never gone one day without talking to each other. They share similar childhood stories. Both of them were overweight for most of their adolescent and teenage years. Neither one of them were asked to prom. Neither one of them had a boyfriend until they were in their twenties. Neither one of them had ever even wore a bikini until last year. It's easy for Tasha to be friends with Janet. Janet already understands her.

Last week, Tasha overheard Michael talking to one of his frat brothers, asking him about the best place to purchase an engagement ring. She was so excited; she immediately called Janet and asked her to meet her for drinks.

"Traffic was horrible! I'm sorry it took so long." Janet plops down in the booth, placing her keys and cell phone on the table.

"No worries, I'm just happy that you're here!" Tasha is beaming with excitement.

Janet eyes her friend suspiciously. "Did we win the lottery or something? Why are you so doggone excited?"

"Michael is going to propose to me next month!" Tasha does the *Single Ladies* hand gesture. "I'm about to be somebody's fiancé! Can you believe it?"

Janet rolls her eyes. "Yes, I can believe it. Michael has always been ready for that sort of thing."

"What do you mean?"

"I mean it's just known around the gym that he was on a hunt for a wife. Looks like he found him one." Janet smiles.

"Really? You're going to totally downplay my moment just like that?"

"What? I don't mean to downplay your moment. I'm happy for you. Just make sure it's what *you* want."

"It is what I want. I love him, but you already know that."

"Wasn't he talking about getting a promotion and moving to Texas? What are you going to do if that falls through? Just up and leave?"

Tasha starts massaging her temples. "If he's my fiancé of course I'm leaving, wouldn't you?"

"Not just like that. You're going to drop everything you have going on here to chase him?"

"Whoa! Like what is really going on? When did getting engaged and moving for new opportunities become a bad thing? Weren't you talking about getting out of Mississippi just last week?"

Janet takes a swig of the sweet tea the waiter has placed on the table. "Yes, I was. That's different though. I would only move if it was the next step in my career."

"I'm in the medical field, I can get a nursing job anywhere. That's not why I called you here. I don't want to talk about my job, I want to talk about my joy!"

"I'm happy for you friend. I really am. We both are looking for happily ever after. I'm glad that you found it."

"Are you? I can't tell."

Janet grabs Tasha's hand. "Don't take it like that. I just want you to be careful with Michael. He's older and he's looking for a young, hot wife. Only you know what the two of you have. I just have to do my job and look out for you."

Some of you are going to swear that Janet is a certified hater. Janet's actions can be viewed from two perspectives. One, she can be celebrated for being honest about what she knows about Michael and calling her friend out about being ready to drop everything in the name of love. Two, she can be criticized for not being on board with Tasha's exciting news, and being somewhat confrontational during their conversation.

For the sake of positive intent, I will say that Janet is right about her suspicions of Michael. I will say that she is 100% on the money with her observations. Now what? What kind of friend would you say she is? I would applaud Janet for saying what a lot of people wouldn't say...not to your face anyway. When someone tells us that they are engaged or their significant other is about to propose, our normal reaction is to congratulate them. We certainly wouldn't go into a debate on why they shouldn't get married. Not unless we were true friends and we knew without a doubt that the engagement might cause a problem down the road.

Sadly, I've seen many friendships unravel behind scenarios such as this one. Tasha may feel slighted because Janet isn't happy for her. What kind of friend wouldn't be happy for you if you just told them you were about to get engaged? Tasha may feel that Janet is jealous. Let me say this, everybody isn't jealous of you. Some people are just being honest about who you are and what you're doing.

The point I would like to make is, if you are woman enough to call someone your friend, you should be woman enough to consider her opinions about your life. The problem is, a lot of women are friends with people they don't trust. A lot of women are friends with people they feel are jealous of them. A lot of women are friends with people and they don't value their opinions. I will say this again, if you are woman enough to call someone your friend, you should be woman enough to consider her opinions about your life. That does not mean that you have to agree with them. That does not mean that they are right and you are wrong. It simply means that you should *consider* what they are saying. After all, why would a friend want you to fail? Why would a friend want you to be unhappy? Why would a friend cause you pain? If you have had bad experiences with the people that you call friend, it goes back to the point I made in the introduction of this chapter. You should not use that word so freely. Some women are your home-girls, people you grew up with. Some women are your associates, people you hang out with from time to time. Some women are just women, people that you know from a period of time in your life. Stop calling everyone your friend. Stop trying to turn haters into friends. I don't know about you, but I do not desire to have frienemies. I would rather have real, authentic people around me.

The more we trust ourselves, the better we can trust others. I trust myself. I trust myself to make good decisions about people and I trust myself to put the right people in my circle. If you aren't good to yourself, you can't identify when someone else isn't being good to you. Get clear about who you are and the type of people you want in your life. You will then attract the type of people that belong in your life; thus, creating a formula for genuine friendships.

Chapter 10

"I don't need a friend who changes when I change and who nods when I nod; my shadow does that much better."

"I don't need a friend who changes when I change and who nods when I nod; my shadow does that much better."
-Plutarch

We're on the topic of friendships. We're discussing the types of behaviors that would be categorized as healthy friendships, and the types of behaviors that would label a friendship as unhealthy or toxic. If you're in your thirties, you just have a little bit more on your plate than you did when you were twenty-something. Maybe you've started a family, maybe you have a new husband, maybe you're trying this entrepreneur thing out, and maybe you're knee-deep in your professional life. No matter what you do or don't have going on, I'm sure you don't have time for any kind of relationship that's not going to enhance your life.

Some time ago when Twitter was really popping, I read a quote that really stuck with me. Twitter used to be the place to grab a nice quote. Anyway, the quote read; "you cannot be friends with someone who wants your life". After further research, I discovered that this is an Oprah Winfrey quote. What she meant was, you can't be friends with someone who 's not fulfilled in their own life. You cannot be friends with someone who wants to be you. Those types of friendships just leave too much to be considered. Is this person your friend because they truly enjoy your friendship, or are they friends with you so that they can get the things that you have? If you're a mover and shaker, a person who has a lot going on, you just don't have the mental capacity to handle this kind of arrangement.

This is 30

Remember when we were younger and we wanted to dress just like our friends? Remember when we all wanted the same hairstyle? Remember when we felt inadequate if we didn't have the same toys or gadgets that our friends had? This was a growing period when we were trying to figure out who we were. Eventually, we started to create our own personalities and only do the things that we wanted to do. We started to wear the kind of clothes that we wanted to wear. We started to wear our hair in styles that made us feel pretty. It wasn't about anyone else.

There are some women who have not grown out of that stage. Sadly, some women are still stuck in that teenage mindset. You may not notice the signs until it has become a problem in your friendship. A grown woman isn't going to call you and say, "let's where our red skirt tonight". No, she's going to be a little more manipulative and conniving with her actions. She's going to shop in the stores that you shop in. She wants to be the first one to purchase something that she knows you want, just so that she can rub it in your face. If you love to carry Brahmin bags, she's going to find the most exclusive Brahmin bag out there. If you have a thing for nice extensions, she's going to research the best hair and fail to tell you about it. If you've been thinking about getting a new job, she's going get a new job and keep it a secret like it wasn't a big deal. It's exhausting being friends with this kind of woman.

....

Pam and Jennifer have been friends since they were in middle school. When they were younger, they lived just two houses down from each other. Pam was the only child of a wealthy, older couple and Jennifer was the youngest girl of her family. Their parents were always away working or on some exotic trip, the girls spent countless days and nights together. They would often have sleepovers on school nights, and even spend whole summers together. Although they both came from money, they had very different personalities and aspirations. Pam was the scholar. She graduated top in her class, and received a full ride to any college of her choice. Jennifer was the social butterfly. Everyone loved her.

She was perky and pretty and cool. Most of the time, she wasn't even trying to be that way.

Pam was super serious, and super focused. She knew exactly what she wanted to be, and she knew how to get there. After high school, Pam went off to UCLA and Jennifer attended a local university that offered her a full athletic scholarship for track. They never lost touch with each other. They were not able to see each other everyday, but they certainly made an effort to see each other once or twice a year. Eventually, both girls graduated and began their careers. Pam became a Pediatrician and Jennifer returned home to help her father run their real estate company. Because she was an only child, Pam always knew that she wanted to have a big family. She couldn't wait to get married and have children. On the other hand, Jennifer couldn't keep a man. Not because they didn't want her, she didn't want them.

The older they got, the more Pam started to become agitated with Jennifer's actions. When they were younger, it wasn't uncommon for both girls to want and get the same things, but Pam had outgrown that type of behavior. Even though they lived miles apart, Pam started to notice a characteristic in Jennifer that she wasn't too fond of. At first, Pam thought she was reading too much into it, but slowly and surely, more signs started to appear. For instance, anyone who has ever come in contact with Pam knows that she enjoys fine art. While her friends were getting cars and jewelry for graduation, she was getting twenty thousand dollar paintings. One day, Jennifer was on SnapChat, showing off her new kitchen and living room décor, and there and behold was a Jeff Koons painting sprawled across her living room wall. She innocently showed everything else in the living room and didn't even acknowledge the painting.

On another occasion, Pam surprised her family by coming home on an odd weekend. She thought that she'd surprise Jennifer by stopping by uninvited. There in the driveway was a brand new Range Rover. Pam had bought herself a Range Rover a few months ago for her thirtieth birthday. Sure, there are thousands of Range

Rovers being made every day, but why wouldn't she say anything about it? It was like the painting. If you knew your friend was a total Jeff Koon fan, why wouldn't you tell her about this great painting that you bought?

Pam decided to enjoy the trip and not ruin it by being confrontational. She had not seen Jennifer all year and she didn't want to start an argument over material things. Pam removed her seatbelt and walk towards the front door. She rung the doorbell and stepped out of view.

Jennifer was on the phone. She peaked out of the door, didn't see anyone and went back inside. Pam rang the doorbell again. She really got a kick out of messing with Jennifer. Again, Jennifer opened the door. This time she stepped all the way out, fuming with her hands on her hips. "Who in the world is playing…"

Pam could not believe her eyes. Jennifer had to be about four or five months pregnant, and she was wearing an engagement ring on her left finger. "Oh my God."

Jennifer dropped her phone in the chair and ran to hug Pam. "Girl! I didn't know that you were in town. I just talked to you and you didn't say one word! Come in, come in!"

Pam stood still. "Um, are we forgetting to address the elephant in the room? When did you get a Range Rover, when did you get pregnant, and when did you get engaged? I'm so confused." Pam was more confused than ever. Jennifer hated kids, she went through boyfriends like shoes, and she said trucks were too big and bulky.

Jennifer rubbed her growing belly. "Yes, we have so much to catch up on!"

Pam started to get angrier by the minute. "Why are you acting like we haven't spoken in months? I talked to you three times last week. I talk to you every single week. You haven't mentioned any of these life occurrences to me."

Jennifer sat down in a wicker chair. "Well, we wanted to wait until we were out of the danger zone to tell people about the baby. And of course I'm getting married if I'm having a baby. The truck, well I'm having a baby and I need a bigger car."

Pam stood looking at her childhood friend. It's like they had warped back into teenagers. Jennifer had a reputation for always trying to "one up" her friends. She already had such a glamorous life, no one thought that she wanted to be someone else, but now Pam wasn't so sure of Jennifer's intentions. "This is just so weird to me. I saw the painting on Snapchat a few months ago. What was up with that? Why didn't you mention it?"

"Because I didn't want to. I don't have to tell you every little thing about my life." Jennifer's attitude now matched Pam's.

"You're right, but you should mention these things just in conversation. The only reason you wouldn't is if you were purposely trying to prove a point."

"Prove a point? We are thirty years old, why would I need to prove anything to anybody?"

"Why would you imitate someone's life? Stranger things have happened."

"Imitate your life? Okay you have the same truck, but the last time I checked, you don't have a husband or a baby."

Pam laughed an angry laugh. "But you knew that I wanted to get married and have a family. It's like you're warping your life into my life. You've never wanted these things!"

"I have a great life, why would I want your life? So a person can't get pregnant or get engaged because you haven't reached those milestones yet?"

"If you had called and said something, it would seem perfectly harmless. Weird, but harmless. Keeping all these secrets, and sneaking to get the things that I have or want seems…creepy!"

"So you're jealous because I have the life that you wanted. Pam, I've never labeled you as the jealous type."

"I'm not jealous of someone who's intentionally trying to imitate my life, my hopes, my dreams! You need help Jennifer. You really have a problem."

"I don't have a problem. You're just jealous." Jennifer gets up and slams the door, leaving Pam on the doorstep.

....

There's nothing wrong with being inspired by your friends. There's nothing wrong with your friends turning you on to a new product, a new brand, and a new lifestyle that you weren't accustomed to. The problem with Pam and Jennifer is, Jennifer sits back and observes the things that Pam has or that Pam wants. Her number one goal is to beat Pam to the punch or do it better.

These are young girl games, and a woman in her thirties should not find herself investing in a friendship with a person like Jennifer. We must learn to love our friends and see them as an extension of ourselves. Our society has programmed us to think it's okay to love to hate people. I do not desire to be around someone who wants to imitate my entire life. It's not flattery, it's downright creepy. If you are a woman who is imitating your besties, please stop! Stop thinking that your friends are flattered that you are warping your life to resemble their lives. Let me let you in on a secret; they are talking about you to someone else. They are annoyed by your behavior. They don't understand why you won't be yourself. People who are secure and in love with themselves will never act this way. If you are the imitator, change your thinking; change your ways. If you are the person being imitated, run! Seriously, you do not have to run, but you definitely need to establish some solid parameters and have an honest conversation with your friend.

Chapter 11

"Women cannot complain about men anymore until they start getting better taste in them."

> ## "Women cannot complain about men anymore until they start getting better taste in them."
> ### -Bill Maher

I hate to use so many references to social media, but it has become the method in which we communicate and the method in which we interact with others. I don't know about you, but I am so tired of waking up in the morning and going to sleep at night to "I hate men" posts. Seriously, we have all hated men at some point in our lives, but when the same person is talking negatively about the same guy day in and day out, I just want to scream..."*leave him already!*"

As grown women, we have to learn the art of controlling our emotions. There is no need to post negative comments about your significant other if you're going to be back with him in two days. As a matter of fact, there's no need to post *anything* about your significant other, because it's simply none of our business. We don't want to know when he bought you a dozen roses. We don't want to know when he failed to pick you up after work. We don't want to know that it's date night. We don't want to know that he didn't buy you anything for Valentine's Day; it's simply none of our business. When we post personal details about our lives, we welcome the world into our relationships, whether good or bad. We give people permission to have an opinion, and we give people permission to judge.

....

Allison is a loner. She works as an Accountant by day and as a Facebook stalker by night. Allison is a woman who believes in order and routine. Each day, when her workday is finished, she sweats it out at the gym for an hour, stops by Publix to purchase items for dinner, and then heads home for the night. She's never been a super sociable person. Even in high school and college, she was always labeled as the shy, pretty girl. Until recently, Allison was single. One of her co-workers convinced her to start dating a "Mr. Right Now" until "Mr. Forever" shows up. Meaning, he's a player. Allison knew he was a player when she agreed to start dating him. She just wanted someone to spend time with.

Allison told herself that she wouldn't fall in love with Chris. This was supposed to be a "no strings attached" situation. After six months of casual dating, Allison found herself where she didn't want to be, in love. Initially, she thought that Chris would come around, and that they would go out every now and again. To her surprise, he totally romanced her. Chris sent flowers every week. He paid attention to the things that she talked about. He would call her every night to see how her day was. He would even attend church with her sometimes. The casual situation turned serious really fast.

One night, Chris was over making Allison's favorite dinner. She was in the living room watching old Martin episodes, scrolling through Facebook, and sipping on a bottle of wine. Chris's iPhone starts buzzing in his jacket pocket. He calls for Allison to bring him his phone. She reaches into the pocket, pulls out the phone, and almost chokes on her wine. There is a picture of a newborn baby on his screen with the word "Baby momma" as the caller.

Allison sits the wine glass down and slowly walks into the kitchen. She hands Chris the phone. He smiles at the picture and hurriedly answer the phone. Allison is leaning against the counter, her hands are folded across her chest, and she's bubbling on the inside.

Chris puts down the kitchen utensils and leans against the counter space farthest from Allison. "Hey girl! What's going on?"

He continues to have a full conversation. After about ten minutes, he ends the call and starts back cooking.

Allison stares blankly at him. "Are we not going to address what just happened?"

Chris looks confused. "What do you mean?"

Allison lets out a nervous laugh. "You have a newborn baby?"

Chris glances at his phone and then starts cheesing like a Cheshire cat. "Oh yeah, I thought I told you about that. She had the baby last week. Remember I told you I was visiting a friend in the hospital?"

Allison walks closer to him. It feels like she's in a Twilight Zone. "You said you were visiting your friend in the hospital. You didn't say you were visiting your baby mama."

"Same thing." He's giving Allison in a non-apologetic glare.

"It's not the same thing, are you crazy? I never knew that you were involved with someone else."

"I'm no longer involved with her. We were involved, she got pregnant, and now I have a beautiful daughter. What's the problem?"

Allison runs her hands down her face. Her mouth is dry. Her heart is pounding in her chest. "Put the utensils down Chris. I can't believe you're acting so nonchalant about something so serious. Let's just call it a night."

"Really? I thought we were just casually dating? Isn't that the word you like to throw around?" He using his fingers to make air quotes when he says casually.

"Casual or not, that's kind of something that you should mention." Allison walks towards the door. She holds it open it and motions for Chris to leave.

Later that night, Allison posts a status to her Facebook wall:

I am soooooo over grown ass boys pretending to be grown men! What kind of man would fail to mention that he has a newborn baby? You'd think that after six months of dating, you'd be comfortable enough to mention that sort of thing. I swear, I'm about to go on a blocking spree. I'm sick of men!!

When she woke up the next morning, she had over fifty comments. Many of the women told her to leave Chris alone and wrote equally damaging remarks about men. Allison knew that Chris was following her on Facebook. She was hoping that her comment hit him dead smack in the ego. Last night, she did block his number so that he couldn't call her. She needed to get over him and she needed it to happen fast.

Allison went about her normal routine that day. She posted a few other cryptic posts on Facebook, but didn't make any personal references. She even reposted a couple relationship quotes on Instagram. Around three o'clock, her receptionist walked into her office carrying a vase full of fresh flowers. Allison already knew whom they were from. The note read that he was sorry. He also said that he wasn't looking for a serious relationship but he didn't mean to hurt her feelings. He said that he wanted things to go back to the way they were when they first met.

Allison didn't know how to stop having feelings for him. She didn't know how to pretend that she wasn't hurt. Everything in her told her to trash the flowers, change her number, and run for the hills. Instead, she snapped a picture of the flowers, posted them on Facebook, and quickly unblocked Chris's number.

....

Ladies, it's always dangerous to get into a casual situation with a man when you really desire to be in a committed relationship. I don't care how big and bad you think that you are, it's just hard. Now, if you're the type to date multiple men, you may not have the time or energy to invest the kind of emotions that would get you emotionally caught up. But if you're dating one man with the hopes of having a serious partnership, you're walking in the danger zone.

How many of you can relate to Allison's Facebook rant? Even if you have never verbally assaulted someone on social media, I'm sure you've run across your fair share of posts that are laced with the same venom. Because this is a transparent collection of thoughts, I must admit that I have typed out a rant or two or ten when Twitter came on the scene. I was in a new relationship. We were having new relationship issues. My emotions were all over the place, and I let him have it! Those are not my proudest moments, but I learned a valuable lesson from that time in my life.

When I see women falling into the same emotional tunnel, I sympathize with them because I know what it feels like to have your heart set on fire. I wish them well. I wish them peace. Most of all, I wish for them to grow from their experiences. It pains me to see women post a rant one night and then post Emoiji hearts the next night. Why, because the "breakup to makeup" has stunted the growth. Sometimes you have to sit in the fire and burn and let pieces of your skin fall off before you can feel what you are doing to yourself. Although you are in a relationship with someone, you must still take ownership of the treatment you are allowing to happen. I don't know about you, but I'd rather go through the pain of heartache one time rather than feeling that same heartache over and over with the same person.

To be clear, let's not confuse hurt with mistreatment. You're going to go through some trials and tribulations when you're in a relationship. At some point, you're going to feel disappointment. At some point, you're going to feel sadness. However, mistreatment is when you are allowing someone to take you down through there. The relationship is draining you emotionally and spiritually. It may even be causing changes to your physical appearance.

Find your center. Your center is your internal safe place. No matter what's going on in my world, no matter how crazy things may be, I know that I will be okay if I can retreat back to my center. It's like being at war. It's like being on the front line in war. Guns are sounding off, people are falling by the wayside, the enemy is coming for you, but there's an ironclad fence and green pastures on the other side of the battle. You may have to fight to get there, but once you've made it, you're safe from harm. You may have a few broken bones and a few bruises, but you're okay.

Chapter 12

"We always think that we'd be happier in some faraway place; as if you could catch a plane to a state of mind."

> **"We always think that we'd be happier in some faraway place; as if you could catch a plane to a state of mind."**
>
> **- Robert Brault**

I *must* have been planning my entrance from my mother's womb. I *must* have been anticipating what the first days on this new planet would be like. I *must* have been figuring out what kind of child I was going to be. If not, where did I get this crazy obsession? I have always been a planner. I have always been a dreamer. When I was in elementary school, I couldn't wait to get to middle school. When I was in middle school, I couldn't wait to get to high school. When I was in high school, I couldn't wait to get to college. When I was in college, I couldn't wait to get my first job. When I got my first job, I couldn't wait to start making big bucks. There is always something else to look forward to. For me, there is always something else to achieve.

The mind is a powerful, time machine. It has the capability to allow us to surpass our now and focus on the next. I lost my son when I was 31 weeks pregnant. Even though I thoroughly enjoyed every single minute of my pregnancy, my mind was definitely focused on what life was going to be like once he was born. In my mind, I had picked out his first Christmas outfit, I had planned his first birthday party, I had taught him how to walk, and I had traveled the world with him. When the doctor told me that his heart was no longer beating, I grieved all those moments as if they had really happened. To everyone else, he was just a baby in my stomach. In my mind, he had already lived so many years. It took some serious soul searching for me to realize that I had created an alternate life in my head. Although you may not have experienced something of that magnitude, I'm sure you mentally zip past your "now" more times than you can count.

....

Sharon's 2002 Honda Accord decided to stop working in the middle of five o'clock traffic. Uncle Bobby, who is the most reliable person she's ever met, came to the rescue. With embarrassment running through every vein in her body, she put the car in neutral as he pushed her out of the middle of the road. It took him about an hour to get the car to start up. The clouds were darkening, and echoes of thunder could be heard in the distance. It was during times like this that Sharon absolutely hated her life. She spent all day working a job that didn't even cover her monthly bills, drove a car that had its' own personality, and had to rush home to turn in a paper she hadn't even started on. The last thing she needed was to be on the side of the road for an extra hour.

Uncle Bobby got the motor to turn. She thanked him, gave him a twenty for his trouble, and sped down the interstate. She made her exit off the interstate and just like magic; the sky opened up and drenched the earth in warm, cascading teardrops. The wipers on her car needed replacing, so she had to stop at a gas station until the rain let up. Out of habit, she started thinking of excuses to tell her professor about why her research paper was late. Sharon was in her last semester of graduate school. That alone is what got her through the day. She knew that she very close to having a very different life. She planned to move out of state, get a new apartment, get a new car, and get a brand new life. There was nothing particularly wrong with the life she has now, she just dreamed about having more and doing better. The only time she was afforded the opportunity to think was during times like these. She worked two jobs while going to school full-time.

Sharon is apart of a really big family. She's the youngest of seven children. Her aunts and uncles have a lot of children, so there's never a shortage of people to hang out with. She just doesn't make time to do any of those things anymore. She wasted a lot of time in her twenties partying and being irresponsible, which pushed her to getting her Bachelor's degree in her thirties. For some strange reason, she thought that she'd have a job waiting for her once she graduated. That was definitely not the case. After graduation, she started working with the State Department making twelve dollars an hour. With student loans and credit card bills, she had to get a second job. She didn't qualify for any of the jobs she applied for, which is why she's enrolled in a Master's program. She's hoping that her work experience and new degree will help further her career. Partying wasn't the answer, graduating with her Bachelor's degree wasn't the answer, maybe happiness is on the other side of this new degree and this new move.

True to form, Sharon makes it home and produces a last minute assignment. She flips on the TV, hops into bed, and sleeps the night away. This is her routine for the next four months. Eventually, Sharon graduates with a Master's in Child Development. She is offered a director's position in Huntsville Alabama. It's a twenty thousand dollar raise. Sharon happily bids farewell to her family and prepares for the life she's been waiting to live.

Sharon quickly realizes that the life she's envisioned might be a little different than her reality. The new apartment is three hundred dollars more than her old apartment. The new car comes with a new four hundred dollar note. The new job comes with a new six-day work schedule. She's forced to get a second job at the mall to balance out her budget, and leave a little money for savings. Sharon finds herself back in the same routine, living life the exact same way.

....

We have to learn to appreciate, love, and be grateful for our now. I'm not sure if it's human nature, or I'm just crazy, to envision what life will be like once we do this or do that. There is one thing that I know to be true; we are never ever really satisfied. There's always going to be something that we strive to accomplish. There's always going to be some place that would be better than we are right now. We will never reach true fulfillment until we learn to be one hundred percent present and grateful for what's standing in front of us. No matter if it's an old vehicle, or a tiny apartment, or a low paying job, or a ring-less left finger. Think back to those times that you rushed through. I would give up a pair of my best shoes to have just one more day on the beautiful campus of Alcorn State University. I would give up everything I own to feel my son's tiny feet playing kickball with my bladder at three in the morning (rolls eyes). I would love to travel back to high school. Don't you miss those days when you could sleep all day and party all night? Don't you miss viewing the first of the month as the time when your parents got paid and not the time of the month when you go broke? But we rushed through all of those moments.

Happiness is not waiting in some faraway land. True happiness lives on the inside of you. It's already there. You just have to stop daydreaming about tomorrow and focus on today.

Chapter 13

"A wise man once said nothing."

"A wise man once said nothing."
-Anonymous

When you are on the verge of greatness, it's natural to want to share your good news with everyone around you...right? I'm not talking about things that have already been accomplished; I'm talking about the "I'm about to" news.

"I'm about to get my PH.D. I'm about to move to another state. I'm about to dump this zero. I'm about to level up..."

True enough, you may have every intention to do all the things you promote, but sometimes life happens and things fall through. Or, you could be one of these social media celebrities posting things for likes and attention with no real intention of completing the things you've put out there. For the sake of exercising positive intent (a strategy I like to use as often as I can) let's assume you really are trying to make these things happen.

About three or four years ago, I wrote this awesome little book. Someone advised me to use social media to pump up the anticipation for potential buyers. So I did. I shared bits and pieces of the cover image; I even put out a tentative release date even though I hadn't got confirmation from the publisher. Then, I decided *not* to publish the book. I felt it needed more work, I wasn't pleased with the edits the editor made, and the whole process just turned into something that made me nervous and uneasy. I became fearful of releasing a piece of work that I felt wasn't a true representation of my work, but I already had so many people congratulating me and anticipating the release. I have been writing fictional stories since I was a small girl. It was not out of the norm for me to publish a book; most people are probably wondering why it has taken me this long. So there was pressure to produce a great body of writing, and the pressure to meet the irresponsible deadline I set for myself.

I think (using positive intent) we promote the things we are working on because we are looking for support from others. We all need a little push sometimes, and sometimes we think that over-sharing or putting it out there will help us stay motivated.

Gabrielle has been working towards obtaining her PH.D for four long years. She will start the program, and then she will take some time off to do other things. To give her a little credit, Gabrielle has a very demanding job. It's difficult for her to find the time to take care of day-to-day responsibilities. Adding school in the mix just further complicates her schedule. Gabrielle doesn't have plans to actually use her PH.D; it's only going to serve as a nice introduction when people say her name.

Gabrielle is competitive by nature. Her competitive spirit has definitely helped her land massive accounts at work. If Gabrielle thinks that someone is out-working her or about to pull a move that may be celebrated by others, she'll work day and night, sunup to sundown to swipe the victory for herself. It's not so much as a jealousy thing; she just wants to win by any means necessary. She often measures her success by the success of women she aspires to be. Last week, Gabrielle was in the supermarket with her mother and she ran into an old classmate who is doing very well. Kelly wanted to know about Gabrielle's job and her husband and her children. It was an innocent conversation where two people catch up with each other. But not for Gabrielle, she rattled off ten different projects that she was involved in (that she hadn't even started or thought about for years). She made sure to tell Kelly that she was in school finishing up her PH.D (she's not currently enrolled). Kelly was very impressed with Gabrielle and invited her to speak at a big time women's conference. Kelly gave Gabrielle her email address and asked her to type up a bio, being sure to mention all of the incredible projects she's involved in.

Gabrielle felt like a fraud. She didn't exactly lie. Well, she might have lied about how far along she was with all the projects she mentioned…but they were real! There was no way that Gabrielle could have those things up and running before the conference. She would either have to cancel her appearance or totally fib her way through the entire event.

....

Gabrielle likes the attention she receives when she completes a task. Gabrielle enjoys being congratulated. That same opportunity would have been there once she had completed the projects she spoke so eloquently about. Now, Gabrielle risks the chance of being viewed as a liar, or smooth talker. She risks the chance of being exposed. She risks the chance of watering down all of her real accomplishments, due to people measuring her success on fabricated achievements. Although I had every intention to publish my book, I did enjoy the feeling I felt when people viewed me as an author. This was a goal of mine since I was a teenager. I felt a sense of pride when I saw my name printed across the book cover. I did feel a sense of completeness, even though the project wasn't complete. This book will be released very differently from the first book I wrote. I will not breathe a word until the proof is in my hands. We learn from our experiences, and I learned a very important lesson about publishing.

An article written in 2009 further explains our intentions when it comes to announcing our plans before we accomplish them. "People who talk about their intentions are less likely to make them happen. Announcing your plans to others satisfy your self-identity just enough that you're less motivated to do the hard work needed. Once you've told people of your intentions, it gives you a 'premature sense of completeness'. Since both actions and talk create symbols in your brain, talking satisfies the brain enough that it neglects the pursuit of further symbols." (Derek Silvers)

Experiences have taught me to move in silence. Anything can happen. I've seen people talk about their hopes and dreams and someone will plant a negative thought/seed into that person and their dreams never take flight.

The older I get, the more I understand the importance of allowing your actions and successes to speak for you. I no longer seek the approval of others; therefore, I am not concerned with updating people about my every move, my every accomplishment. As thirty-something women, we should seek to be pleasing to ourselves. We've had our moments of being on the stage, being subjected to who we should be and the definition of success according to other people. Now, it's time for us to create our own definition of success. It's time for us to wise up and shut up.

Chapter 14

"My best successes come on the heels of failure."

"My best successes come on the heels of failure."
-Barbara Corcoran

Women are creating businesses left and right. Technology has changed the way we create companies, making it easier than ever to create innovative start-ups. Perception is the ability to see, hear, or become aware of something through the senses. Many people perceive entrepreneurship as a way to make fast money. Perceptions are based on our surroundings and our experiences. I see everything as entrepreneurship. I cannot walk through the mall without seeing a pair of Spanx and wondering how Sara Blakely feels to have her idea turn into the phenomenon that it is. I cannot use my iPhone without wondering how Steve Jobs felt after it hit the market and changed the way we communicate. When I'm traveling, I cannot call an Uber without wondering what Travis Kalanick and Garrett Camp were really thinking about when they visualized how to modernize the way we travel. These things are on a large scale due to my surrounding, the literature I read, the conferences I attend, and the people who are inspirations to me. For some, the neighbor who has started a successful online boutique is their definition of entrepreneurship. For some, selling luxury hair on Facebook is their perception of what it means to be an entrepreneur.

These days, entrepreneurship can be viewed in many forms. You'd be surprised at what people are inventing and selling. Some of it is amazing, and some of it is a little nuts. No matter what type of business you are admiring, please know that it is hard work and it's not as easy as people make it out to be. Going back to the word perception. Using photography, videography, and words, we create our own perceptions. In business, we call it branding. I am the CEO of Schoolhouse21. We use branding to paint a picture of our company. During a recent Meet and Greet, a woman cried and said, "This is what I've been waiting on". Don't get me wrong, it's a fun company to work for, but it's also hard work. We have fun creating marketing campaigns and presenting our ideas to the world, but we also burn the midnight oil trying to meet deadlines and write proposals. You won't find any of those things on our social media feeds, but that doesn't mean it's not happening.

That can be said for the people you are watching. You are front and center for their success, but they most likely did not grant you entry to watch them fail. You have to be very careful about how you perceive things. If you are interested in becoming an entrepreneur, I would advise you to get off social media, pick up the phone, and have a real conversation with several business owners. The next story will be based on one of the many times when I felt like giving up.

....

As an education consultant, my primary job is to travel around the state to assist public school teachers and students with high stakes assessments. Meaning, it is my job to ensure the teacher's know how to prepare the students for the test, and ensure the students know the content. Five days a week, I will travel four to five hours a day. Unlike most jobs, I did not have any training from my current employer. As a consultant, you are the expert and it is your job to know what you're talking about. The school districts are paying you big bucks to turn their schools around.

I started my career as an education consultant at the tender age of twenty-seven. At the time, almost nine years ago, you could count the number of twenty-year old consultants on one hand. There were not many. I found myself in a profession that was demanding, stressful, yet very rewarding. I loved every minute of it.

In the consultant world, you are paid by the number of days you work. You can easily make from seven hundred to one thousand dollars a day. My very first contract was in another state. The contract was for over one hundred days. This is a dream come true as a consultant, you're not at a different school every day and you're not sweating bullets worrying about if you're going to have money coming in from month to month.

On the first day of the contract, I entered the school to meet the administrator. There were two older consultants with me. The administrator took one look at me and immediately formed a very negative opinion about the quality of work she thought I could provide. In the administrator's eyes, I was entirely too young to be a consultant. After the meeting, I felt nervous but I was excited to get to work. Later that night while preparing for the next day, my supervisor called to say that she was going to move me to another school at the request of the administrator. I felt devastated and defeated. Even though the decision didn't affect my income, I felt embarrassed and incapable. I called my significant other and cried on the phone. I told him that I was quitting; I told him that this wasn't the job for me. He told me that I was NOT quitting and that I was going to go to the other school, prove that I belonged in this field and prove that I was qualified to do the job. That's exactly what I did. The new school was in the same school district. By the end of the year, the teachers from the school I had been moved from were requesting my resources and assistance. Ain't God good?

....

Nine years later, I've founded two education companies and a nonprofit organization. It's not how you begin, but how you finish. People who see me today will only see my successes. They will not see all of the failures I've encountered. As a mentor, I try to communicate that failure is just a necessary steppingstone. There's no way I would be who I am today had I not failed so many times.

There's no secret formula. Be ballsy. Be persistent. Never, ever give up. Never, ever let anyone out work you.

Chapter 15

"Growth and comfort do not coexist"

"Growth and comfort do not coexist"
-Ginni Romelty

Ideally, we would love to be able to grow and chill at the same time. No mam, that's not going to happen. If you're comfortable, you're not growing. If you're going through each day and you never meet any kind of resistance, you never have the urge to do more, you never feel incomplete, you never feel like you're not doing what God has called you to do…you're not growing. It's as simple as that. Your mind is in the exact same place as it was last year and the year before that.

I started teaching right out of college. You would think that I was prepared to be an English teacher since I was an English Literature major, but I wasn't. I thought that once I got the job, everything else would be a piece of cake. No, I had some growing to do. I literally went home every night to study the same material I had assigned to my students. It's not as if I didn't have a clue about the content, but I wanted to know the material backwards and frontwards. Dealing with teenagers, you better know that stuff backwards and frontwards and sideways too. I'm just saying! It was tough. During my stay in Atlanta, my friend girl and I started an online magazine. That required growth. We had to learn about establishing a business, how to write sponsorship proposals, how to hire the right people, how to oversee interns, how to keep our readers engaged, as well as a host of other things. I definitely was not comfortable. We were so uncomfortable that we nixed Rochelle Nicole Magazine and started other ventures. We weren't uncomfortable because we did not want to learn new things; we were uncomfortable because sometimes growth will show you what you're not ready or prepared for.

This is 30

On the other hand, have you ever met someone and immediately see so much potential in him or her? Does it bother you that they refuse to better themselves? As a mentor and woman in business, I had to learn to allow people to step up to their growth at their own speed. A person will not and shall not grow until they hear that tiny voice inside of them that screams, "It's time." As a matter of fact, you don't have to worry about when the voce will appear. When it's time for you to grow, you will become so uncomfortable with the world around you that you will break out of every binding chain just to have freedom.

....

Rhonda is a hair stylist at a popular hair salon in the city. The owners are a husband and wife duo that have been around long enough to vamp up enough clientele to keep every stylist busy and booked. The salon doesn't really specialize in any special service; they pretty much can do whatever the client requests.

Rhonda hasn't pursued anything outside of hairstyling. She started braiding her friends hair when she was in middle school, she graduated to gluing in weaves once she reached high school, and once she made it to college, she was pretty good at just about everything that dealt with hair, chemicals, and extensions. Rhonda majored in Chemistry just because she had a love thing for the sciences when she was in school. She was fascinated with the human body, cells and reproduction, and anything dealing with the creation of things. She did not have any plans to actually use her Chemistry degree; it was something she did to make her parents proud. Both of her parents were college graduates, and even though they supported her desire to be a stylist, she knew deep down that they wanted her to respect the tradition of the family.

A typical day at Hair Magic, the salon where Rhonda worked, was like the atmosphere at any urban salon. The clients spent an obscene amount of money on their hair. Jerry and Toni had their systems in place. The clients belonged to the salon, not each individual stylist. Although the clients had their picks, Rhonda was not allowed to book her schedule with new clients of her own. She had to run her schedule by the front desk clerk to make sure there were not any walk-ins or clients that had requested her through the salon. It kept the stylist busy, but it also took a lot of control out of their hands.

Over the years, Rhonda became more and more interested in chemical processing and the benefits of having natural hair. She was able to use the information she learned in undergrad to further research her findings. After researching and following natural hairstylists, Rhonda approached Toni and Jerry about starting a natural hair sector of the salon. She wanted to be one hundred percent in charge of all clients who wanted to adorn their natural hair. Toni and Jerry liked the idea of adding a new service to their menu, but they did not like the idea of Rhonda being the only stylist to offer natural services.

Rhonda felt like the couple was going to take all of her ideas and research and figure out a way to benefit them, so she stayed quiet about the things she knew and the natural procedures she practiced. She would often invite women to her home so that she could try out new techniques without Toni and Jerry criticizing her every move. Rhonda's home hair care became so popular, she found herself having more clients at home than she did at the salon. Everything in her told her to just start her own salon and step out on faith. She would take four steps forward, but fear would always creep back in and send her back to Hair Magic.

It was becoming harder and harder for Rhonda to pretend that she was happy. When a client would schedule a perm, she would fume about it for hours. She wasn't allowed to tell them how damaging the products were. Toni and Jerry had made it clear to all the stylist that chemical processing and weaving were their money makers and they wanted the stylist to market those services as much as possible.

One day, a mother brought her fifteen-year-old daughter into the salon. She said she was tired of fighting with her natural hair and she wanted Rhonda to perm it so that it would be more manageable. Rhonda wanted to tell the lady that she had so many options outside of perming it, but she knew she would be reprimanded. After seeing how upset the daughter was, Rhonda decided to educate the mother and daughter on alternatives for straightening coarse hair without putting chemicals in it. Toni sat lurking in the back as Rhonda finished her spill. The mother wanted Rhonda to use the products and techniques she spoke about, but the salon did not carry those items. All of the items Rhonda needed were at home in her makeshift kitchen salon. The mother scribbled down the products and thanked Rhonda for her honesty.

After they left, Toni came charging around the corner with Jerry on her heels. They wanted to know why Rhonda did not offer the mother the chemical service. She tried to explain that the daughter had Eczema and that the chemicals would further agitate her skin. They didn't want to hear it. Toni asked Rhonda to pack up her things and take a leave of absence. Initially, Rhonda wanted to beg for her job. She thought about her light bill and her cable bill and her mortgage. Just as quick as those thoughts came, so did the vision of people lining up to come to her natural salon. The anxiety faded and a seed of excitement was born. Rhonda packed up her things and hummed a new tune as she exited the salon.

....

Growth and comfort cannot and will not coexist. It's like oil and water. It's like Batman and the Joker; they don't get along. They don't want to be in the same room with each other. Your fears will opt for you to choose comfort. By choosing growth, you're telling your fears that they have to hit the road, and they don't like that. They would rather lurk around in your mind and convince you that what you have is enough, that what you're doing right now is enough. They, your fears, will paint some pretty scary pictures, but don't be fooled. The more you grow, the more you learn, the less you will hear from Brother Fear. He'll always be hanging out in your mind, but when you have grown to a certain point, when you are confident enough to walk in your God given abilities, his voice won't have the same power as it once had.

Chapter 16

"Wisdom is nothing more than healed pain."

"Wisdom is nothing more than healed pain."
-Robert Gayle Lee

When you know better, you do better. If you don't do better after knowing better, you will stay stuck in a painful, stagnant place. Obviously, I love to write. I love to write fictional stories. I love to pen memoirs. I'm becoming more and more interested in picture books. I love to write using smooth, Paper Mate pens. I love to write on fresh notebook paper. I love to write on napkins. I will sit down and doodle just so that I can have a reason to hold a pen. I'm obsessed. More than anything, I love to write personal journal entries. There's something about writing down raw, unfiltered emotions. When I'm crafting a book, I have to be mindful of my language, my grammar/punctuation, and my audience. When I'm writing in my journal, it's just my thoughts and me.

There have been so many painful moments that have happened to me in the last few years. Moments that threaten to change who you are on the inside. Moments that will turn your heart sour. Moments that will permanently alter the way you view life. In the midst of those storms, all I could see was pain. I couldn't see the joy of tomorrow. I saw pain. I felt pain and I heard pain. Luckily, I have each of those moments recorded in my journals. When something bad happens to some people, their natural reaction is to call someone or cry. My natural reaction to pain is to write about it. When I got the telephone call that my grandfather had unexpectedly died, I immediately went to the Notes app on my phone and wrote about how I was feeling. I did the exact same thing when six months after my grandfather died, my cousin called me to tell me that my father was found unconscious at his home. He died about two hours later. After the ultrasound technicians told me that my son's heart had stopped, I didn't write. I went through thirty-three hours of labor, and twelve whole days of silent despair before I penned one word. That moment was harder than the others. It was harder for me to put my feelings into words, because for the most part I was numb.

Today, I am able to go back to those moments, and other less painful moments to read about my journey. Through the written word, I can sense when I was having a hard time, and I can sense when the clouds started to part. Journaling may not be for you, but I urge you to find something that serves as a healing mechanism for you. It cannot be someone, not unless that someone is God. There's not a human on earth that can help you heal those dark craters in your heart. Why, because then your healing is based on a person they have the ability to help your healing or stunt your healing.

There will come a day when you wake up and the air is sweeter, you can breathe a little better, and your eyes can see past the pain. That is when you are on the road to recovery. During those times is when it is important to pay attention to yourself and everything around you. That is when you will grow a grey hair and gain a new branch of wisdom.

....

The quietness of the cold room felt comforting to Brandi. She wasn't in any rush to turn on the heater or grab a blanket from the hall closet. She wanted to sit in her misery and feel every ache and every sharp pain. It had been approximately five hours, twenty-two minutes, and three seconds since she had gotten the call that her father had died. She could hear people bustling about the house. She could hear pots banging and kitchen cabinets closing. Why do folks always think that a warm meal will ease a broken heart? After trying to be polite and tell people that she wasn't hungry and that she didn't need anything, she simply locked herself in her bedroom and retreated to the bench in front of the massive bay window.

Everything on the outside was still the same as it was five hours ago. The blanket of snow hugged the ground with winter fierceness. The frosty air looked thick and damp. The music from Carl's Juke Joint could be heard from miles and miles away. They were still jamming, and life was still happening. Brandi smiled at the irony of it all. The people at 325 Sycamore were mourning the lost of a legend, a giant in human form. The people down the street at 331 Sycamore were mourning the life, all of its' twists and turns and hills and valleys. Brandi swallowed down tears, and they swallowed shots of Bourbon.

Brandi's phone buzzed, which indicated that she received a text message. Her best friend, Jody, texted to let her know that she was in the living room if she needed her. Brandi thought that was strange. She hadn't even noticed that Jody had pulled up, and why would she want to hang around her family when she didn't know them that well. Jody was a coworker that turned into a friend. Most of their interactions were away from family.

Over the next few days, Jody kind of hung back while being right there. It was very strange. She knew when to talk. She knew when to be silent. She knew when to step in and offer a helping hand, and she knew when Brandi needed to do the task on her own. After the funeral and after everyone had retreated back to their normal lives, Brandi asked Jody about her concerns.

"How did you know what to do for me? It was kind of weird. How did you know when I needed to be left alone? How did you know I needed you to pick out the coffin?" Brandi wiped away tears as she spoke.

Jody reached out to offer Brandi a tissue. "I don't have parents. You probably notice that I never talk about them. They died in a car accident about seven years ago. I just did for you what I wished had been done for me. When it first happens, you don't want to talk. Hell, your heart doesn't work so it's pretty hard to make your mouth form a word. When it was time to pick out a casket, I didn't care if it was hot pink or burnt orange. I didn't want my parents in a casket at all. I didn't want the responsibility of peering into a box, feeling which cushion would be better suited for their lifeless bodies."

It all made perfect sense to Brandi after hearing Jody's explanation. There was nothing weird about what she did. It was actually pretty remarkable. She took all of the pain she went through and turned it into a beacon of light for someone else.

....

Wisdom does not come with age. I know a bunch of old fools. Wisdom comes from *learned* experiences. If you have gone through one thousand experiences and you didn't learn anything from any of them, I would not label you as a wise person. All it takes is for you to learn from one experience. Those experiences and those lessons are designed to help you along the way. There are people who go through the same thing forty times. Why, because they haven't learned what it is God is trying to teach them. Most of the time, you won't know when you've grown a branch of wisdom until it shows up to help someone else. I can honestly say that despite what I have gone through this year, I am happier than I have even been. I'm at peace. I've grown in ways that I never thought possible, and I know that my experiences have imparted a great deal of wisdom into my life.

Chapter 17

"Do you want to meet the love of your life? Look in the mirror."

"Do you want to meet the love of your life? Look in the mirror."

Byron Kate

What does it mean to love you? The self-love movement has become a thing. With women empowerment songs, self-help books, and ridiculously funny memes, it would be difficult to find a woman who cannot rattle off a self-love saying or quote. They have entire shows dedicated to women finding themselves and loving themselves. So why are women still unable to truly love the person that stares back at them in the mirror?

There are many reasons why self-love is at the bottom of the totem pole. For one, we live in a beauty-obsessed world. Everybody is a 10. Every celebrity is a 10. Cosmetic surgery is more affordable than it has ever been before. Getting a little lipo done is as normal as saying you're about to go purchase a new pair of shoes. People will not clutch their pearls or lose their minds if they found out you went to get a little nip and tuck. Not to mention that we are constantly watching photo-shopped celebrities on our television screens and mobile devices. These days, it's easy to mold yourself into someone else. With the download of an app, a swipe of an index finger, you can have a perfect body, a perfect nose, whiter teeth, thinner thighs, and a flatter belly. If you use these apps and filters, does that mean that you don't love yourself? No. There's nothing wrong with using a filter or an app to enhance some of your features, but there is a problem with someone who cannot show herself to the world without relying on these tools.

Although we have more information than we've ever had before on how to love ourselves, women are not internalizing these teachings. I can read a great book on how to love myself, but if I'm still allowing my man to disrespect me, I'm not applying what I've learned. I can listen to Joel Osteen until I'm blue in the face, but if I still treat myself worse than I treat other people, what am I really learning from these sermons? It goes back to what I said earlier in the book, you cannot and will not see the changes you wish to see until you commit yourself to doing the work. Learning to love you is not an easy task. Especially when everything and everyone around you is telling you that you're not good enough as you are.

....

Ellen is a stay-at-home mother of five kiddos. Ellen's husband is an investment banker. He travels about half of the year. The family has learned to rely on Skype Facetime, and other communication platforms. Ellen would love to have her husband home with her every night, but she's gotten accustomed to their lifestyle, and she wouldn't trade that to have Rick looking in her face everyday. He's a nice enough man. They've been married since the year they graduated college. Rick came from a big family and he wanted to continue the legacy. Ellen wasn't too keen on having five children, but she was raised in a Christian household, being submissive to her husband is a top priority of hers.

Ellen was always very athletic. She played tennis for the majority of her adult life. She stopped playing after Morgan was born. Morgan was child number four. She had her when she was thirty-five. In her mind, that was it, their family was complete. Rick begged and pleaded with Ellen to try for one more boy. He felt that having three girls and two boys would balance out their family. It would also give their son, Brice, a brother to grow up with. Ellen gave in and gave birth to Hunter just last year, at the ripe old age of thirty-eight.

Ellen use to love herself. Lately, she just couldn't stand the thought of looking at herself in the mirror, and her confidence was at an all time low. It's like her once toned body decided to fall apart after Morgan was born. She no longer have the time or the energy to work out. Taking care of five children isn't an easy job. They always need her. She can't remember the last time she had a day to just relax and enjoy a glass of wine. She can't remember the last time she left the kids at home and went to the mall to shop for herself. She can't remember the last time she took a bath and didn't have someone interrupt her to ask for something.

Rick didn't understand, his solution to the problem was to get a nanny. He didn't see below the surface. In his eyes, if Ellen needed more time to herself, she should hire a nanny. If Ellen did not like the way she looked, she should go visit a gym or a plastic surgery center. He just wanted his happy-go-lucky wife back. He wasn't home to witness the day-to-day duties of raising children; he didn't understand how tiresome it was. Even if she hired a nanny to help her with the babies, she still had to deal with the demands of her teenagers. They needed to go here, they needed to go there, and they needed her to make this, or handle that. Most days, Ellen wished she could run away and never come back. She loved her children, but everyday she felt like she was drowning. Everyday she felt like she woke up to please other people. No one really noticed if she was having a bad day. No one really noticed if she was sick. She was invisible.

....

We cannot be love to other people if we have not learned how to love ourselves. There should never be a point in your life when you feel it is okay to love someone else better than you love yourself. There was a time when Ellen loved and valued who she was. During those times, the family flourished. Now that Ellen is having issues practicing self-love, it seems as if the sky is falling. She wakes up everyday in a full panic because she is overwhelmed and maxed out.

As women, we are the anchors for our families. They depend on us. They look to us to be a guiding light. How can you be the nurturer for your family if you have not learned how to nurture yourself? There is absolutely nothing wrong with taking some time for you. Ellen should have called Rick and told him that he needed to get home. She should have told him that it was an emergency, call 911. She should have told him that is was a life and death situation, because it was. His wife is drowning and he doesn't even know it. His wife is withering away, her spirit is lost and the walls are crashing in. As mothers, as wives, learn how to communicate with your spouse. Stop trying to be superwoman. Actually, you should return the cape. Return it to whomever gave it to you and tell them that you don't want it back. Seriously, we have to learn to lean on our helpmates. We cannot do it all. We've been raised to feel like we should be able to do it all. We've been raised to feel like it's our jobs to do it all. Somebody lied! It's okay to ask for help. It's okay to say, "I feel lost. I'm losing myself. I need a break."

I don't care who you marry and whom you birth, no one can love you better than you can love yourself. It starts with you. The way you love yourself is the way others will love you. If you're okay with beating yourself down, they won't see a problem with doing the same thing. Say your name. You were you before you became all these other things. Treat yourself like you're somebody.

Chapter 18

"If you can't figure out your purpose, figure out your passion. For your passion will lead you directly to your purpose."

"If you can't figure out your purpose, figure out your passion. For your passion will lead you directly to your purpose."

Bishop T.D Jakes

I am living on purpose. I am clear about who I am and what I should be doing with my life. My brother said something that resonated in me not too long ago. He was at my office, helping me put together a few computer desks. He looked around the training room and said, "Your ass was always trying to play school. We wanted to wrestle and play momma and daddy, and you wanted to play school." There will be moments on your journey when you question your next step. You will question if you are walking the right path. If you are on the right track, there will be confirmations sent your way. Him saying that was another tally mark for me. I remember being a little girl and wanting to play school. I played school with my dolls. I played school with my cousins. When my mother had my younger brother, I played school with him. There was always something in me that wanted to give myself away in the form of teaching.

I went to being a classroom teacher, to a consultant, to a business owner. I must admit, the higher I climbed on the ladder to success, the more I started to question my direction. If classroom teachers made more money, I probably would have stayed in the classroom. I love interacting with students. I love to teach literature. I love to create fun projects. I love to teach teenagers how to be independent thinkers. I've always been about my coin, so staying in the classroom wasn't an option for me. I knew I wanted to stay in the education field, I knew I wanted to work directly with teachers and students, and I knew that I wanted to determine my own salary. Being a first tear teacher is tough. I didn't really have anyone to take my hand and show me the way, so I started a company that filled that void. As I traveled around the state, I realized that not only is it hard to be a new teacher, it's hard to be a principal and staff your school with quality people. I started a company that filled that void. Because I am clear about who I am and where I'm going, all of my ideas are centered on my purpose. I love to write, I aspire to be a New York Times Bestselling Author. Even through my writing, I'm still teaching.

Many people get lost in making a living and making a life. Your job is what helps you make a living; your purpose is what will help you make a life. You may hear people throwing that word purpose around and you can't figure out what it means to live on purpose or live a purposeful life. The simplest way for me to explain is to ask you what you enjoy doing. What would you do for free? What have you always been interested in? What do you do well? That is your purpose. If you aspire to be an entrepreneur, you have to creatively figure out how to monetize your gift.

....

Anna was born to be a southern girl. After college, Anna took an internship with Saks Fifth Avenue. She majored in marketing and advertising. Living in New York City was difficult for Anna. Although she was learning so much, she couldn't quite adapt to the weather or the northern hostility. She rarely went out to enjoy the city. During her time there, she focused on her work and dedicated herself to moving up in the company. She quickly became a force to be reckoned with. Because of her eye for details and her warm personality, Sak's made Anna VP of Company Relations. Her job was to create company events and initiatives for the employees, partners, and investors. Anna loved every minute of it. She never woke up and dreaded going to work. She was always excited about the next day, she was always eager to get started on the next project.

After working for Sak's for seven years, Anna returned home to Charleston, South Caroline. Her mother had fallen ill and her father needed a helping hand. For the first two years, Anna struggled with finding a job. She got a job with a marketing agency in the city, but it wasn't something she enjoyed doing. She never felt challenged. She never felt like she had to try very hard or push herself to a certain limit. The job was easy. The duties were things that she did her very first year at Sak's as an intern. She searched high and low and just couldn't find a job that made her feel the way her previous job did.

One night, after helping her dad put her mother to bed, she decided to confide in him. She had hidden her aggravation from him because she didn't want him to feel guilty about asking her to come back home.

"Dad, I'm unhappy." Anna drew her knees to her chin and dropped her head in her lap.

"I've been waiting on you to say something about that. I could tell you were unhappy here. You don't have the same spark as you used to have. Is it the country life? Do you miss the fast-paced city life?"

"No, I hated living in the city. I'm unhappy with my job. I hate Mondays. Actually, I hate every day of the week. I have to talk myself into not calling out. My boss is clueless and when the work day is over, I feel like I've wasted eight hours of my life."

"What would you like to do? What did you do in New York that was so grand?"

Anna's eyes lit up. "I coordinated these out-of-the-box events for Sak's. Once they told me who the event was for, I had the creative control to do whatever I wanted to do."

"You can't find something like that here?"

Anna's spark faded. "No, I've looked."

"Well why don't you create it yourself?"

Anna was puzzled. Her dad was a worker bee. He spent his whole life clocking in to work for someone else. She couldn't believe that he was pushing her to start her own business. "Are you serious?"

"Yes, I'm very serious. Life is short. I went to watching your mother be the life of the party, to bathing her like she's four years old. It's time to do what you've been called to do. I know money is tight for you. We have some savings that we could loan you to get started."

For the first time in two years, Anna felt like she was on the right track again. She slept a little more peacefully that night.

....

I'm very passionate about women walking in their purpose. As a woman, we have so many other barriers and hurdles to jump over, walking in your purpose gives you the fuel you need to keep going. My mom has been working a 9-5 since I can remember. I am constantly on her about working for herself and finding something she truly enjoys doing. We only have one life. We should use our time to impact the world with our gifts.

How do you find your purpose? Find a quiet place. Make a list of all the things that you would do for free. List your hobbies. Now make a list of the things that you do well. Make a list of the things that people often ask you to do for them. Circle it. Put some big stars around it. Throw some glitter on that thing. Hang it up. Put it on your vision board. Now figure out how you can do what you love to do, what you do well. It seems like it would be a no-brainer. It seems like everyone should be walking around doing only what they love to do. Well, there's a thing call life and responsibilities, but it's possible. Create a timeline, create a plan, and get to work.

Chapter 19

"If you can't fly then run, if you can't run then walk, if you can't walk then crawl, but whatever you do you have to keep moving forward."

> **"If you can't fly then run, if you can't run then walk, if you can't walk then crawl, but whatever you do you have to keep moving forward."**
>
> ## Dr. Martin Luther King Jr.

Life is hard. I don't think I'll find one single person to debate me on that statement. The older we get, the more responsibilities we have. We also start to lose people that we love. We are wiser. We have more demands. The older we get, the more we want. Around thirty-something is when you start to look back and look forward to figure out what's next. What will your forties be like? How are you setting yourself up to be successful? How will you learn from your mistakes and do things differently? All those thoughts are important. All those thoughts are things we should think about. However, it's hard to think about tomorrow when you're not sure you're going to make it past today.

There are some women who are really struggling out here. There are some women who need help. Not just financially and emotionally, people are struggling mentally. Mental illness is a real disease. We should treat it as such. There are women out here who are taking their lives. When we were younger, we didn't really identify suicide as a result of mental illness. The old people just said that he/she took the easy way out and were headed straight to hell. I won't get into the religious thing on that topic. Believe what you will about where they are going in the afterlife, I'd like to concentrate on how to help them while they are here.

There are some people who are just lazy and they can't catch a break because they are not putting themselves in a place to catch a break. You will never be successful if your only desire is to sit on the couch everyday. On the other hand, you have some women who can't catch a break because life is constantly beating them down. For some reason or another, they can't get on their feet. They can't feed their families. They can't cloth their kids. They can't afford to put food on the table. They can't even afford the luxury of buying sanitary napkins. Their backs are against the wall and they can't find a way out. A lot of women who commit suicide are actually pretty spiritual. Some, not all, find suicide as a way to be closer to the one person who can fix all of their problems.

....

Bonita passed a piece of bread to her two daughters who were sitting in the backseat of the car. They had been living out of their car for about a week now. Bonita got fired from the factory two months ago. They lived in a small town. If you weren't working at the factory, you had to travel about an hour to find work. Bonita had two small girls. Their father's were never present in their lives. Because they were not school age, Bonita had to foot a daycare bill. She was receiving assistance from the state, but her old boyfriend messed that up for her. The people found out that she was lying about the number of people staying in her house, and the amount of money that was coming in. Her benefits have been suspended for about a year now.

Lulu, Bonita's youngest daughter suffers from seizures. It's hard to find someone to watch the kids because people are skeptical of caring for a special needs child.

Regardless of what Bonita faces, her kids are her everything. She was a child who was forced into the foster care system, so she fully understands what it's like to have parents who can't take care of you. She always wanted more for her children, but a few bad mistakes have followed her throughout her adult life. When she was a teenager, she got caught up in helping some girls steal money from their part-time job. She didn't get a chance to go to school, and having her record tarnished with the criminal charge hasn't helped her land the most ideal jobs.

She was employed with the factory for three years. Honestly, there were times that she missed work because she was chasing some guy around town, but the day she got fired was the day that Lulu had a really bad seizure. Lulu has hospitalized for two weeks. Even though she had a doctor's excuse and a hospital release form, HR didn't want to hear it. They felt that it would be better if Bonita focused on caring for her young child.

Rent was due at the beginning of the month. Bonita was already two months behind. After losing her job, there was no way she was going to be able to catch up. In the middle of the night, her and the girls packed up their Honda Element and drove to the nearby RV Park. She knew the landlord would be around to collect rent the next morning, and she didn't want to face the embarrassment of being kicked out in broad daylight.

So here they are. Cold, eating pieces of dry bread, and trying to figure out their next move. Despite how bad things are, Bonita is grateful that she has her kids with her. She was abused and mistreated as a foster kid. That will always be her first priority. Making sure they are all together and making sure that her children know that she will never abandon them, no matter how tough their situation is.

....

Someone once said, "throw your problems in a pile with everyone else's and you will quickly want your problems back." If I were in Bonita's situation, that would be the end of the world. I couldn't fathom having to live out of my car with two small children. But she's doing it and she is strong enough to find a silver lining. How many people do you know that would be grateful for anything in that situation?

Women, we are strong. We can do remarkable things. No matter where you are in life, no matter how hard it may be…hold on. Continue to have faith, continue to be grateful, and continue to fight. You should never settle for a life that you know you were not put here to live. Things may not be going the way you hoped they would. You may not be where you thought you would be at this age. The stars may not be aligning. But your time is coming. Like the quote said, you may wish to fly, but if it's not your season to fly, I need you to walk. If your legs are broken from life and you cannot walk, you better get to sliding. Just keep moving. Just keep pushing forward.

Chapter 20

"Amateurs sit and wait for inspiration, the rest of us just get up and go to work."

"Amateurs sit and wait for inspiration, the rest of us just get up and go to work."
-Stephen King

If someone sold inspiration, I would have bottles tucked in every corner of my house. Don't you love the feeling you get when an idea jumps into your brain and completely takes over your whole body? When I'm inspired, the sun seems to shine a little brighter. When I'm inspired, my heart is smiling and the weight of the world doesn't seem as heavy. I have learned to listen to my inspiration and pay attention to the things that inspire me. Sometimes, I'm caught off guard and inspired by the most unlikely things. Other times, I have pinpointed a place or a song or a person that can help me get to the inspirational core that I'm searching for.

When I started writing this book, the idea to use quotes and storytelling to empower women hit me like a ton of bricks. In the beginning, I stayed up day and night pouring every word I had into this manuscript. Then it happened…the inspiration was gone. If you are a creative then you understand what I'm talking about. No matter how hard you try, you just can't get excited about what you're doing. It's like you're stuck. When I was younger, I would let the lack of inspiration keep me from completing a task. As I got older, I realized that if it's something that needs to be done, I'd better get to doing it regardless if the inspiration is there or not.

....

Kristen is a clothing designer. She attended a fancy design school in California, took an unforgettable internship, and return home to open her own boutique. While in school, Kristen had to design based on what the curriculum called for. If they were studying a certain technique, that's what she had to produce. During her internship, she was asked to design using the inspirational boards that were provided to her. The clothes were for magazine photo-shoots so she always had to stick with the vision of the photographer and creative director.

Kristen was beyond excited to open her own boutique. During the first four years, she designed the type of clothes that she always wanted to create. She would spend every waking hour designing and sewing and producing colorful masterpieces. Soon, her clothing line and boutique took off. Meaning, it became highly successful. She was forced to create patterns and outsource the sewing. She was forced to hire a team of designers to help her cater to the demands of her customers and clients. Although her business was on a different, larger scale, she missed the days of sewing in her kitchen while watching an episode of Dr. Phil.

The demands of the business soon sucked the inspiration from Kristen. She found herself relying heavily on her design team, without offering much leadership. She was making more money than she had ever dreamed of, but she was often left uninspired. She became so aggravated with the whole process, she thought about selling the business so that she could do other things. It's not that she didn't love her business; she just felt that she had topped out. She felt like there was nothing else she could create that wasn't already being made.

Kristen's husband sensed that something was wrong. For her birthday, he booked her two trips. One trip was to California to her old design school. The other trip was to New York, to visit the company she had previously interned for. Kristen spent two whole weeks talking to former professors and supervisors, interviewing students who were enrolled in the program. She even visited some of the old restaurants and landmarks that inspired her to draw. Just being around the fast-paced environment lit a spark in her. On the last night, she looked through her portfolio and realized she had designed twenty dresses while on vacation.

After returning home, Kristen realized that she's not going to be inspired every day, but it's up to her to take a break from the day-to-day to create opportunities where inspiration can flow.

....

We cannot sit around and postpone our dreams because inspiration decided not to show up. If we did, we'd never accomplish anything. We have to be diligent in our pursuit to keep going even when we have no idea where we are going. During the quiet times of your life, during times when your mind isn't crowded with to-do's and concerns, inspiration will come knocking on your door. Be open and ready.

Chapter 21

"It is easier to find men who will volunteer to die, than to find those who are wiling to endure pain with patience."

"It is easier to find men who will volunteer to die, than to find those who are wiling to endure pain with patience."

-Julius Caesar

Patience is a virtue, or so they say. You've figured out what you're good at, you've clearly identified your purpose in life, now it's time work, work, work, work, work. Did you sing Rihanna's song when you read that part? Let me be clear, you're going to be doing a lot of work, but you probably won't see the return for some time. Whether you're publishing a book, or starting a new business, or waiting on an engagement ring. You're going to be tested with the patience of five thousand men. It's going to seem as if you'll never get to where you're trying to go. It's going to seem like once you take five steps forward, you're pushed ten steps backward.

These days, most people want whatever it is that they're working on to come easy. Many people will quit way before they get to the finish line. I remember having people come up to me and ask me about being a consultant. People have heard that consultants make good money, so they wanted to know what the qualifications were and how to go about securing a position. I'm an open book. I try my best to help others because someone helped me. As women, it is our duty to pull up the next woman. To date, I've only had one person (who inquired) to actually complete the steps needed in order to be a consultant. The life seems glamorous, and the flexibility is attractive, but once people hear about the process, they start dragging their feet. The same can be said about a lot of things. To write a book, you have to make yourself sit in front of a computer for hours and hours each day. You may not feel like it, but you absolutely have to stick to a writing schedule. I wanted to quickly publish a book, but when I rushed it, it didn't turn out right. Remember the first book that I mentioned? I chose not to publish it because it was a rush job.

Exercising patience can be uncomfortable, whether it is personally or professionally. We are learning new information at rapid speeds. We want the Internet package that produces the fastest loading times. Everything is about quick, fast and in a hurry. It's not surprising that we expect everything to be that way.

....

Tonya and Lamar have been together for two years. They met online on a Christian dating website. Tonya made sure that she was very specific when writing her bio. She told her potential mate all about her likes, her dislikes, what she did for a living, and her relationship aspirations. She was practicing celibacy and she preferred to be married and have at least one child before she turned thirty-five. She was thirty-four and her thirty-fifth birthday was only nine months away. Tonya had dedicated her life back to the Lord after suffering an extreme heartbreak with the man that she thought she was going to marry. He led her on for four years only to dump her for another woman.

Lamar loved Tonya. She was driven, adventurous, smart, spiritual, and funny. She was the total package. The only thing that he didn't like about Tonya was her constant nagging about marriage and kids. He wanted to be married and he wanted to have children, but he didn't want to rush into it just because she was turning thirty-five years old. To a certain extent he could understand her dilemma, her clock was ticking and she didn't want to be raising a toddler in her forties. He understood all of that, but he just wasn't going to rush into anything just to check one of her goals off the list.

For Christmas, Lamar bought Tonya a new Apple Watch and a pair of Chanel earrings. He had seen how mesmerized she was by the earrings when they were browsing through the Chanel store late one night. She said that she could never imagine spending that kind of money on a piece of jewelry. Lamar couldn't wait for Tonya to tear open the box on Christmas.

Christmas night, they ate dinner, they sang songs, and they cuddled by the fireplace. Lamar held out Tonya's two, neatly wrapped gifts and handed them to her. Her eyes became the size of saucers. She started clapping her hands and stomping her feet against the floor. At first, Lamar thought that she had somehow peeped into his closet and seen the gifts. I mean she was totally freaking out. Then it dawned on him that the earring box was the same size as an engagement ring box. He felt like a complete ass. In that moment, he knew that Tonya thought that he was proposing to her. He grabbed both of her hands before she could tear the box open.

"Babe, calm down. Before you open your gifts I just want to say something to you."

She squealed. "Just say it!"

Lamar placed his hands over his face. "An engagement ring is not in that box. We're not getting engaged...tonight. It's going to happen, just not tonight."

Tears filled Tonya's eyes. "Why not? Did I do something wrong?"

She was making him feel worse and worse as time went by. "No, no, you haven't done anything wrong. I just think that we need a little more time to get to know each other."

She frowned. "Get to know each other? Wow. I'm speechless."

"Why don't you go ahead and open your gifts. I just didn't want you to think I was playing some kind of weird emotional game with you."

"But you are playing an emotional game with me. I told you what I wanted before we even started dating. I've wasted enough years of my life waiting on a grown boy to propose. If you're not ready, then I think it's time we go our separate ways."

Stunned, Lamar held up his hands in protest. "Hold on one second. You're willing to throw away everything that we have because I'm not giving you an engagement ring tonight?"

"Absolutely." She sat stoned face.

"So do you love me or do you love the idea of being engaged?"

"I guess it doesn't really matter at this point since you're not ready to be married. It doesn't matter if I love you."

"You are crazy, you know that? I'm so glad this happened. I can't be with a woman like you. You're on some crazy ass timeline and it doesn't really matter what guy you end up with, you just want to hit your deadlines."

"I have zero patience for men who don't know what they want."

....

Tonya was extreme, huh? She lacked patience, and as a result, she didn't have compassion or understanding for her situation. Some women would rather end the entire relationship, no matter how good it was, if they feel like they're going to have to wait too long to reach the promise land.

That brings me to a very important point. Marriage, success, parenthood, and happiness are not something you arrive at and just like that everything is better and brighter. All of those things require patience before you get them and while you're in them. If you view all of those life moments as a place that you arrive at, you're going to be highly disappointment the day after all the hoopla. You'll start thinking, "now what?"

Those life occurrences are beautiful accomplishments, but they're just another important stop on your journey. They are not the end of the journey. In due time everything that your heart desire will come into fruition. Until then, enjoy the ride.

Chapter 22

"Find a purpose to serve, not a lifestyle to live."

"Find a purpose to serve, not a lifestyle to live."
-Criss Jami

"Do it for the Gram!" Actually, let's not do it for Gram. There's nothing that ruffle my feathers more than people faking their purpose. Life Coaches are popping up every two seconds. Everybody is a life coach. Yes, I am rolling my eyes. Everybody is a relationship expert. Yes, I am rolling my eyes even harder. There are some people who are authentically walking in their purpose. Some people have been called to be life coaches and relationship experts. On the other side of that coin are people who want to be popular. The same thing can be said for church folk. It's a little touchy to question someone's religious calling, but pastoring is a big business. Mega churches are blowing up and the First Lady is jet setting around the world in Prada and Fendi. I'm not hating on the designer labels. I'm not saying that you cannot wear designer labels if you are the head of a church; I'm simply stating that some people are more fascinated with the lifestyle than the work.

I blame social media. We've never been front and center of everyone's life as we are now. I can literally read someone's profile; figure out what they do, and read post updates as they describe what a day in their life is like. I'm speaking of the people who give us a daily play by play. If I don't know who I am or where I'm going, I might be inspired by someone else's life. I might think it's cool to be a carbon copy. I might not have a problem deceiving people. It would be great if we could get an alert when we meet someone who is passionate about hustling, and those that are passionate about purpose.

Dr. Tina Rey has been a certified Master Life Coach for about six years. She specializes in entrepreneurship and personal development. Tina started selling insurance when she was twenty-four years old. She became highly successful, and eventually crossed over into real estate. To date, Tina's real estate firm is ranked number thirty-three out of all registered and license firms in the United States. At the time, she didn't have a college education. She was actually a very promiscuous teenager when she was growing up. It is her life's mission to help younger women find their place in the world. She coach women who are on the path to owning their own business.

Recently, Tina's personal assistant created her a couple of social media pages in an effort to get her name and brand out there. Tina would like to have the opportunity to reach more women. She's not a big technology person. While she respects the advancements that have been made for entrepreneurs using social media, she's old school. She'd rather talk to you face-to-face than by DM.

After a few months of training, Tina began to get the hang of her social media pages. She learned how to use hashtags and how to effectively create a brand presence. One day, while searching for life coach posts, she ran across another life coach that she knew. The lady was actually a fraud. She had schemed hundreds of women out of money. The lady was going by a different personal name and business name. If you did not know her, you would swear that she was legit. A few of Tina's clients had invested their money into this woman's investment businesses, only to be notified by the BBB that she was fraudulently collecting illegal investments.

Tina scrolled through her posts and read the comments people left. So many women were thanking the lady for allowing them to be apart of the next "big" investment group. They thanked her for being their coach. From the looks of it, the lady had reposted a lot of images from other life coaches' pages. The whole thing completely turned Tina off. She asked her personal assistant to delete her pages. Tina decided then and there that she wanted to have personal relationships with the women she coached. She did not desire to have Internet fame. She wasn't doing what she does to be commended by celebrities or to gain one hundred thousand followers. She wanted to help the next woman because she remember what it was like not having an education, feeling inadequate, and wanting to have a life that she could be proud of.

....

I've met some pretty amazing coaches and entrepreneurs via social media. This chapter isn't meant to discredit those that are truly doing the work. It's meant to raise your awareness of people who are called to do a thing, and people who are hustling a thing. It won't take very long to distinguish the two.

If you are a person who has created a source of income based off what is popular right now, you may want to reconsider. I'm all about getting the coins, but you want to be successful doing something that will be around for years to come. It's not smart to hop from hustle to hustle. Your credibility will diminish…quickly. If you are providing empowering services to women and you are not the real thing, leave them be. There are a lot of women out here who are clinging on, they are searching for help. I would hate for a woman to seek help from someone who is only concerned with how much money is in her PayPal account.

Chapter 23

"It is not that I'm so smart, I stay with problems longer."

"It is not that I'm so smart, I stay with problems longer."
-Albert Einstein

If I could speak to my younger self, if I could offer her some advice that would totally change the way she views the world, I would tell her to never, ever give up. It may sound cliché or too simple, but I have found it to be the single most important element for a successful business. I have found it to be the most important element for a successful relationship. It's easy to give up. It's easy to move on to the next best thing, but when will you progress if you are constantly starting over? Again, you do not learn so much from your mistakes when you move on quickly. You learn from your mistakes when you sit in the mistake, when you sit in the pain, when you refuse to let go until all hope is gone...and you hang on a little while after that too.

I can recall getting a pretty big consulting contract with a school and having a lot of pressure put on me to help a teacher that had been with the district for over ten years. The administrators did not want to get rid of the teacher, but they couldn't figure out why her test scores were always so low. The administrators could not figure out why the students loved her so much, yet were unable to graduate because of their inability to pass the assessment. Everyone was puzzled.

I was in a different state than my home state so I had to really learn the new curriculum and study this teacher's lesson plans. I sat in on a number of her classes prior to dissecting my findings. This lady was always in the front of the room teaching her heart out. She gave the students everything she had. After digging in the curriculum materials, and viewing sample assessments, I figured out the problem. I stayed with it until I knew without a shadow of a doubt what the issue was. What the teacher was teaching, and what was actually being tested, were two totally different things. Not to mention she was only scratching the surface; there was little to no depth to her lessons. Even though she showed up to school every single day, even though she had really great relationships with each of the students, even though she was well prepared for her activities, she was still missing the mark.

I didn't invent anything new. I didn't discover a secret piece of evidence that no one else was privy to. I simply stayed with the problem until I had a solution; I didn't give up.

....

Patrice was sick and tired of being sick and tired. She graduated from Howard University with a degree in General Studies. Initially she was an Elementary Education major, but she did not pass the state teaching examination prior to graduating so she opted for a general education degree instead. Patrice took the exam four times the summer after graduation. Each time she studied, and each time she failed. There was an alternate route program that she could enroll in, but she had to pass the exam in order to be admitted. Her grandmother was a teacher, her parents were teachers, and she desperately wanted to be a teacher too.

After spending over six hundred dollars in exam fees, she finally gave up and decided to become a teacher's assistant. She satisfied her yearning to be in the classroom, and she satisfied her parents concerns about being jobless.

Seven whole years went by and Patrice never thought twice about what she should be doing with her life. She loved her students; she loved reporting to work everyday. Unfortunately, she wasn't able to pass the exam, but that wasn't going to stop her from fulfilling her purpose.

This is 30

The following school year, a new administrator was hired. He was a stickler about goal setting. He felt that teacher's would be more successful and more bought-in if they were happy with their career growth. Patrice was very nervous about meeting with Mr. Waters. He had an intimidation factor about him. She brought in all of the requested materials and handed them to him and she took her seat. He reviewed each document silently and carefully. He began to ask her how on earth could she have so many education courses on her college transcript, yet graduate in general studies. She explained her predicament with the teaching exam. She explained to him that over the course of eight years, she had taken and failed the exam ten times. He quizzed her on her methods for preparing the test. She answered truthfully. He applauded her for staying in the field even though she wasn't getting paid much, and even though she was more than qualified to be a teacher.

The next week during her planning period, a very sharp looking lady appeared in the teacher's lounge. She told Patrice that Mr. Waters said that her lunch privileges were revoked for the next three weeks. Patrice was a little angry and a little confused. The lady asked her to follow her to the library, so she did. Once they arrived, she told her that she was a consultant from the Washington Department of Education. Mr. Waters had arranged and paid for consultants to come and work with the teachers who could not pass the state examination. Patrice cried through the entire first session. She could not believe someone cared that much.

After two more attempts, Patrice passed her test. Mr. Waters did not wait until the next school year to make her a full time teacher. After Christmas break, Patrice entered the school and found her name hanging on the third grade classroom door. Mr. Waters said she had waited long enough.

....

There is no perfect formula to be considered successful. However, it does take an ounce of courage, a pinch of consistency, a cup of inspiration, and a tablespoon of perseverance. All of the greats will tell you that they just kept at it. One day you will get recognized for a talent you have been doing for years. People don't just blow up overnight. They've been working, you just don't see the work until it's time.

Chapter 24

"Folks are usually as happy as they make their minds up to be."

"Folks are usually as happy as they make their minds up to be."
Abraham Lincoln

When you're happy and you know it clap your hands. When you're happy and you know it stomp your feet. Isn't it a joyous feeling to be happy? I'm not talking about the kind of happy that happens as a result of something. I'm talking about that kind of happiness you feel when absolutely nothing is going on. One would expect to be happy if they just won the lottery, or won a new car. How about being happy because you can smell rain in the nighttime air? How about being happy because you can sense that fall is near by the changing of the leaves? How about being happy because the post office didn't lock the doors until 5:02, allowing you to slip in and mail your car payment? What about those everyday happy feelings? Unfortunately, most people do not wake up feeling happy. Most people wake up feeling troubled or worried. Most people wake up dreading some part of their day.

If you were to walk into my home office, you will find countless books dealing with the control of the mind. I am an emotional person. I don't know if I was born this way or if I made myself this way. I have the power to throw myself into an emotional meltdown at any given moment. I probably should have been an actress. Being an emotional being hasn't always helped me personally and professionally. Personally, I've taken quite a few things out of context and went overboard. I've reacted to some situations in the most emotional charged way possible. I've created a fictional story in my head, painting my significant other in the most negative light. Professionally, I've taken a business decision personal when I shouldn't have. I've made business decisions based on my emotions rather than the black and white facts.

Our mind can create a safe haven or a living hell for us. It's all about learning to curve our thoughts and control our thinking. We have to stop listening to the voice in our head. Rarely does she ever say, "Candace, you got it going on." Mostly, she'll tell me that my arms look big, or that the people in the far corner are staring at me, or that I should be cautious of a certain somebody. I'm not sure how happy I would be if I sat around listening to the voice inside of my head all day long.

....

Zuri is your average, over-the-top woman. Some would call her passionate. Many would call her a loud mouth. She believes in aliens and UFOs, the Lochness Monster, and she has a pretty stern opinion on who killed JFK. She's very much in your face. As a bartender, it's kind of her job to be opinionated. She found a career that would allow her to be herself. It doesn't matter if she shows up to work with bright blue hair, or if her skirt is too short, or if she has holes in her stockings. It's not the ideal job for someone in his or her late thirties with four children, but she loves it.

Zuri is the middle sister. Her oldest sister is a big shot attorney up in New Jersey, and her baby sister is a dentist down in Florida. She's the black sheep of the family. She's the one who had the most potential, but chose to do the least with it. Zuri's always marched to the beat of her own drum. She's definitely a modern day hippie.

It's no surprise that Zuri's family would like for her to do more with her life. It's hard for her to attend any type of family function without getting into a heated argument with her older sister about how she's choosing to live her life. As a result, Zuri does her very best to stay away from them. Her and her kids make do. They're happy with what they have and they don't ask people to fund the things that they wish they had.

This is 30

Zuri's favorite time of the year is summer. Not only can she wear daisy dukes and tank tops, she can walk the four miles to work without having to fight with her teenage kids over who's using the car. On her way out of the door one scorching July day, Zuri received a phone call from her mother. She was weeping so heavily, Zuri could barely make out what she was saying. After asking her mother to slow down and repeat herself, Zuri realized that she was trying to say that Yolanda, Zuri's oldest sister, was in the hospital. Historically, the girls have never gotten along. Zuri was just too different from them. While she felt bad for her mom, she still didn't understand the magnitude of the call.

Zuri's family banned together and all traveled to New Jersey. Zuri stayed behind. Apparently, Yolanda was diagnosed with stage four breast cancer. Zuri didn't really know what to do with that kind of news. Obviously she felt sad and helpless, but she didn't think that a visit from her would make Yolanda feel good. She thought that Yolanda would actually be angry and wonder why a "no life having heifer" like Zuri didn't end up with the breast cancer opposed to someone who had so much to look forward to. Maybe that's how Zuri felt about herself on the inside. Either way, she went about her every day life. She made a point to pray for Yolanda at night and send positive energy her way during the day. After coming home from work one night, Zuri got a very frantic call from her youngest sister. Yolanda had specifically requested that Zuri come and see her. Always the control freak, she even had her flight already booked.

Zuri made it to New Jersey the very next day. She greeted her family members when she entered the Waiting Room lobby. Everyone sat with sunken, sullen faces. Zuri lugged her duffel bag across her shoulder and proceeded down the hall to Yolanda's room. It was exactly what she envisioned. The curtains were drawn, the air was thick, and death was sitting in the chair, waiting for Yolanda to give in.

Yolanda heard the door open. She saw Zuri slouch into a chair, staring her down behind hot pink frames. Yolanda pretended to be asleep. It didn't take long for Zuri to work her magic. She carefully pulled out her crystals and her candles. She opened the curtains and placed the crystals and candles in the windowsill. She pulled out her old, grey mini boom box. She fumbled with the antenna until she found a reggae station. Yolanda could see Zuri start to move her head to the beat. She pulled out a couple of adult coloring books and placed them on the nightstand near her chair. She folded her legs in Indian style as she began to color and sway to the sound of the music.

"What are you doing Zuri?" Yolanda's voice was a whisper.

Zuri bolted upright and put the coloring book down. "I'm sorry, I'll turn the music down. I was trying to liven it up a little in here. It's depressing."

Yolanda smiled. "The volume is fine."

Surprised, Zuri picked the coloring book up and started back doodling. "Oh, okay."

"How do you do it Zuri?"

"Do what?"

"How do you stay so positive despite everything that's going wrong?"

"I just figure that everything is going the way it's supposed to go and we can either fight it or roll with it."

"Sounds simple enough I guess." Yolanda closed her eyes.

Zuri put the book back down and walked over to the bed. "What do you need from me? We don't get along. You called me here for a reason, what is it? What can I do to help you?"

Yolanda opened her eyes and looked at her sister. "You can be happy, like you always are. I just need you to be yourself. I want to go out on a good note. Turn the music up."

....

Don't kill my vibe. Over the years, Zuri's sisters resented her easy breezy lifestyle. In a way, they resented how easy her life was. Although she did not have the things that they had, she didn't desire them. She was not impressed with material things. Zuri was more concerned with being in tune with her happy place. She didn't surround herself with people who didn't understand her, which is why the sisters were never close. Zuri did an excellent job at protecting her peace.

You never know who needs what you have. It can be something as small as a smile. Each day, we make a choice about what type of emotion we will wear. Hopefully, you choose to be happy. It's equally as important to ensure that we are able to maintain that happiness throughout the day. Once you make up your mind to be happy, that's what you will be. It's as simple as mind over matter.

Chapter 25

"How do you find self-love? You dig. You isolate. You ache from being lonely. You heal. You accept. You look in the mirror. You see God."

> **"How do you find self-love? You dig. You isolate. You ache from being lonely. You heal. You accept. You look in the mirror. You see God."**
>
> **-Anonymous**

The road to finding and loving yourself won't always be straight and narrow. Most likely, it's going to be filled with bumps, twists, turns, potholes, and ditches. On any given day, you can read a thousand quotes that tell you to love yourself, to put yourself first, to settle for nothing less than what you deserve. All of that is true, as women, we should definitely tap into our power, but I don't want to think that's it's going to be an overnight process. The first thing that you must do is make up your mind that you're ready for a new life. Until you decide that what you're getting isn't good enough, you're not going anywhere. Another person cannot make you love yourself; it's something you have to want to do on your own.

The next step is understanding what self-love is. When people love themselves, what does it look like? How do you get there? Well, the definition of self-love can differ depending on the person. It's primarily based on your experiences. For one person, practicing self-love can be them deciding to let go of a toxic relationship. For another person, self-love can mean taking better care of herself physically. For someone else, it could be them deciding to stop indulging in self-destructive behavior. We all may have a different end result, but the core of self-love is being transparent with how you are allowing yourself to be treated, and deciding to take the necessary steps to practice self-worth.

If you've been mistreating yourself or allowing other people to mistreat you, chances are they you won't wake up the next day with a different mindset. Meaning, you can't decide to practice self-love and expect to have those changes take effect the next day. Obviously, you've created a habit of unworthiness. Now, you must create new habits. Creating a new habit will take a great deal of effort. Along the way, you'll find it easier to retreat back to your old self. You will wonder why you ever felt you needed to change in the first place. In those weakening moments, you must push forward and hold yourself accountable.

....

The swift winter wind danced on Shayla's shoulders. She wrapped the coat around her thin frame, readjusted her scarf, and continued to hike through the crisp morning air. There was no way she was missing her four o'clock appointment. It would have been much easier to stay inside on a day like today, but she was seeing the progress she was making and she didn't want to do anything to jeopardize her growth.

Shayla had been seeing Dr. Pat for about six months. In the African American culture, it's a little taboo to go and see a psychologist, but she wasn't worried about what anyone thought. At first it was a little strange to sit and tell all of her deepest secrets to a total stranger, but the feeling that she felt every time she left was enough to keep telling and to keep going. She found Dr. Pat at a women's empowerment event. Dr. Pat was the keynote speaker. It seemed like she was talking directly to her when she spoke. She talked about how women put themselves last, how women should learn to love themselves, and how life will always be the same until women learn to use the tools that they have to change their lives.

Shayla left the event feeling inspired and motivated. She needed more of what this woman had to offer. The next day, she emailed the event coordinator and asked her for Dr. Pat's information. The lady gave it to her and thanked her for taking the first step. Shayla hung up the phone and immediately started to research Dr. Pat on Google. She had come in contact with her fair share of women who pretended to be someone they were not, and she wanted to make sure this Dr. Pat was the real deal. Search after search brought up the word "psychologist". As much as she wanted to reach out, she was a little hesitant to contact a "mind doctor". She grew up in the inner city; most of the kids who had behavior problems went to this kind of doctor.

Confused and skeptical, Shayla decided to give it a rest and come back to it another day. It's not that she was going crazy, she just wanted to explore the tools Dr. Pat talked about at the empowerment event. Some of the women at the event had real deal problems. Dr. Pat had them to talk about their issues. One woman was an extreme overeater. She was abused as a child and used food to comfort herself. One woman was a serial cheater. She admitted to cheating on her husband. Apparently she had deep-rooted trust with men. She said that she wanted to maintain control of the relationship, so she didn't attach herself to them. Instead, she cheated on them. Woman after woman told their stories. Shayla found a piece of herself in every single one of them.

After constantly passing by Dr. Pat's information, which was now clipped to a magnet on the refrigerator, Shayla decided to give her a call. Dr. Pat's receptionist answered the call and cheerfully scheduled her a consultation. She asked Shayla to complete an online profile prior to attending the meeting. That night, Shayla climbed into bed and went through each question. Even though they were all open-ended questions, Shayla felt like everything she wrote screamed "crazy as hell". She never viewed herself through those lenses. She had never asked herself the type of questions that were on this form. Nevertheless, she completed the form and anxiously awaited her appointment.

That was six whole months ago. Every week, Shayla met with Dr. Pat to discuss her past, her present, and her hopes for the future. They talked about her daddy issues. They talked about her mama issues. They talked about her inability to maintain healthy friendships. They talked about her need for approval. They talked about her insecurities. They talked about everything. But it was so different than just talking to one of your home girls. Dr. Pat helped her arrive at her own answers. She didn't tell Shayla what she should do step-by-step. That's what Shayla appreciated the most. Those were the tools that she spoke so strongly about that day. Dr. Pat was teaching her how to love herself. So, it didn't matter if a hurricane and a tornado decided to meet for coffee. They would just have to get out of her way. She had an appointment with Dr. Pat. She had an appointment with the new Shayla.

....

Being transparent with yourself is the process of identifying what's *really* going on, taking an assessment of your habits and beliefs, and making up your mind to address those things. But what happens when you know without a shadow of a doubt that you're not equipped to help yourself? You seek the help you need. I guarantee there will be people in your life who don't understand. It doesn't matter if they don't understand; this is for you. There will people in your life that will try to discourage you from growing. Decide that your growth is none of their business. What I've learned in my thirty something years is that when you surround yourself with people who are ankle weights, you can't be surprised when they strap themselves on to your legs and try to pull you down. Why are you so surprised? That's just what they do. When you're on a journey to find yourself, you will always have to isolate. You can't hear what's going on with you if you have all this other loud noise going on. When you're on a journey of self-reflection and self-discovery, you only need to bring one person with you... yourself!

Chapter 26

"Never dull your shine for somebody else."

"Never dull your shine for somebody else."
Tyra Banks

Get those squares out of your circle. As a woman who is flourishing and trying to make a mark on the world, you want to surround yourself with people who have similar ambitions and goals. Surround yourself with people who will encourage you to be your best self. Surround yourself with people who will hold you accountable for bad behavior. Surround yourself with people who will question why you're not utilizing your God given talents. On the contrary, when you hand around the latter, they will convince you that "doing you" is doing too much. People who are not in tuned with their gifts do not want to see you use yours. As a matter of fact, they will be so intimidated; they will do everything in their power to help you fail.

The problem isn't with the people who are convincing you to do less. The problem is with you. You have the power is rectify that situation by choosing better friends. Over the years, I have met so many women who are sitting on their potential. For whatever reason, they are choosing to water themselves down. I'm not saying that another person is totally at fault or that they are the number one reason why a person decides not to do more, but it is a fact that people rise or fall to the level of the people they surround themselves with. Not to toot my own horn, but I belong to the wolf pack. The women that I hang around are wolves. We are goal-getters. We do not sit around and gossip about other women, we are too busy building our empires. The five people that I spend the majority of my time with are all entrepreneurs. We understand each other. We support each other. We want to see each other win. We pull each other up.

....

Erica is an up-and-coming entrepreneur. She recently signed a lease on a three thousand square foot space. Erica is hoping to bring her love for luxury shoes to the market in which she lives. For as long as she can remember, she's always been obsessed with heels and luxury brands. She understands that not everyone can afford to buy shoes from Barney's and Neiman Marcus, so she's bringing the brands to them at affordable prices. Erica is opening her city's first luxury shoe consignment boutique.

Initially, Erica didn't think the process would be as hard as it has turned out to be. She scoured the Internet, bought thousands of dollars worth of shoes, and proceeded to sell them through her Shopify account. After tuning in to countless business webinars, Erica realized that in order to be successful, she was going to have to stop trying the beat the system (IRS) and set up her business correctly. She partnered with a local nonprofit organization that is geared towards helping new entrepreneurs start and run their businesses. Erica incorporated her business, secured a tax identification number with the government, set up a Dun & Bradstreet number, and opened up a business checking and savings account.

She was feeling good! The revenue from her online business was enough to secure the building, pay a few months up, and purchase additional inventory. Erica was on the right track. She spent every single day in her store, trying to get it ready for the grand opening. She didn't have many friends, but the friends that she did have were pulling all-nighters with her. They were there to sweep the floor, label shoes, wipe down cabinets, clean the bathroom, stock inventory, whatever she needed.

Erica's boyfriend was skeptical of her friend's intentions. He thought they were just hanging around because they wanted to be associated with the store. Erica wasn't moved by his skepticism.

Through the years, she's had bad friends. She's had the friends that were jealous, conniving, and full of negativity. Her old friends would never clean a toilet just because she asked them to. No, these friends were different. Their conversations were different. Even though their businesses hadn't reached the level of hers, they each had their own thing going on. They didn't need to be associated with her brand; they had their own brand.

She dismissed his concerns, but day after day he would continue to put those seeds in her head. For some strange reason, he didn't want them hanging around. It's like he wanted her all to himself. On the day of the grand opening, he purposely shuns her friends. He didn't invite them to take photos. He would pull Erica away while she was talking to them. Whatever he could do to create distance between them, he did. Erica noticed his antics but she didn't want to make a scene at her establishment. Later that night, she addressed him.

"Why were you acting that way at the grand opening? I thought you were being rude and controlling."

Shawn laughed at Erica. He continued to play his game, never looking her in the eye. "That's definitely an over-exaggeration. I'm not trying to control you; I just don't think you should be doing the friend thing. You got too much going on."

"I don't know what kind of friends you have, but my friends are very supportive of me and my business."

"Right now they are. What happens when you blow up and you don't have time for them?"

"The same thing that's going to happen when they open their own businesses and don't have time for me. I don't appreciate you trying to turn me against my friends." Erica walked to stand in front of the TV.

"Girl, move out of the way. I'm not trying to turn you against your friends. I'm trying to keep you from getting your feelings hurt when they turn on you."

"Look, I get it. It's hard for women to be friends. It's equally as hard for women in business to be friends. But we are friends and we're going to stay friends. Now, if you want to stay my boyfriend, I'm going to need you to be a little more supportive of the people in my life. My friends actually really like you too. Go figure."

....

In this scenario, Shawn was the character who was casting a dark shadow on Erica. Some men do not understand the complexities of women and their friendships. I applaud Erica for putting him in his place. She stood up for her friends. That's rare. Many times, women feel like they have to choose between their men and their girls. An insecure man will want you all to himself. He will not push you to have a life outside of him. In this case, Erica chose not to downplay her friendships just to make him happy. She's blessed to have a circle of friends who are not only supportive, but who are also just as ambitious as she is.

The older you get, the harder it is to find genuine people. When we were younger, neither you nor your friends had anything. The both of you were on the same level. As you level up in life, you will come in contact with people who are only interested in what you can do for them. It's important to cherish the real, authentic friendships that you do have. I'm a firm believer that we attract the things and the people that match where we are and where we're going. Check yourself, and then check the people around you. Never settle for less than you deserve, and never dull your sparkle to fit in with people who are not going where you're headed.

Chapter 27

"There's a special place in hell for women who don't help other women."

"There's a special place in hell for women who don't help other women."
Madeline Albright

I have a love thing for women who empower other women. It is so very important to me. When I was in high school, my mother worked a lot. We had a lot but it was only because my mother was working night and day to make sure that we had what we needed, and a lot of what we just wanted. I also had a great father and stepfather to help provide for my siblings and me. My mother didn't get her degree until after I had graduated college. (She went on to receive a Bachelor's and two Master's degrees) When it was time for me to complete college applications and go on college visits, I didn't have a lot of guidance. I come from small town USA. At the time, we didn't have nonprofit organizations or youth programs that focused on helping us develop or choose the right path. The college alumni chapters did their best, but it was more about choosing this school over that school than focusing on what was the best college for each student based on their interests, and their aspirations. It would have been nice to have a mentor who offered unsolicited advice based on her life experiences. You know, something real that I could hold on to. One of my all-time favorite quotes is, "be the kind of woman you needed when you were growing up." As I'm working in schools across the state, I am very intentional about choosing young girls to mentor. Even though I turned out pretty good, that is what I needed growing up. I'm not sure how different my life would have turned out, but it's definitely something I could have benefited from.

As grown women, *we* still need mentors. I don't care who you are, there's a woman out there that can help you get to where you're trying to go. Gwen Purnell was everything to me when I started consulting. As I mentioned in a previous chapter, I was a twenty-seven year old young woman, scared out of my mind. She taught me the ropes. She taught me the importance of not relying on one gig, and the importance of not letting a company own your intellectual property. Shelia Smith taught me how to be a badass. She taught me how to be confident in my work and how to never let anyone out work you. She taught me to speak up. Mrs. J. Alexander and Mrs. Suzanne Green taught me how to be a great English teacher. They were awesome teachers. They knew the content like the back of their hands. They taught me to be knowledgeable of what I was teaching. Keith Brown taught me how to be a doer and not just a thinker. He taught me how to work hard. He taught me how to be confident. He taught me how to do business. He taught me how to get that money.

Who do you have in your life that can take you by the hand and show you the way? If you think that you have nothing left to learn, you're not growing. You're probably working a job that does not fulfill you. If you're not open to learning or growing anything new, you are comfortable being right where you are. I'm not comfortable. I'm grateful, but I'm striving for more. To have more, I have to link up with people who can help me get there.

Olivia is shadowing Dr. Odom, the Executive Director of Girls United, a nonprofit who's mission is to give back to less fortunate teens in the metro area. Olivia was partnered with Dr. Odom through a church initiative. Olivia has plans to start her own nonprofit organization one day. She's been shadowing Dr. Odom for about two days, and the lady hasn't been very pleasant. She's not being mean, she's just being very dismissive. Yesterday, she asked Olivia to help sort applications. Olivia was very excited about this task; she thought that Dr. Odom might explain what they are looking for when they chose applicants to be apart of Girls United.

Well, that didn't happen. Olivia found herself in a small room, organizing the hundreds of applications by grade level and last name.

Today, they were going to conduct their second round of interviews. Because the membership process is ongoing, there are always applications to read over and an interview to be had.

When they walked into the room, a teenage girl was sitting at the table. She stood when she saw Dr. Odom. Dr. Odom placed a huge smile on her face and reached out to hug the girl. Olivia was a little taken aback. She didn't think the woman believed in personal contact since she had been acting cold and distant towards Olivia. They went through the interview. The interviewee was brilliant and charming. Olivia was confident that Dr. Odom and her team would ensure the girl was apart of the organization. After she left, Dr. Odom's face went back to its' expressionless mold. She pulled out her laptop and began to type fiercely.

Olivia cleared her throat. "I'm sorry to disturb you but I have a question."

Dr. Odom didn't look up from the screen. "Sure, how can I help you?"

"I'm not a college student. I'm not a child. I'm a grown woman that was partnered with you through my church. I have high hopes of starting my own nonprofit someday. I'm not sure if I've done something wrong or not, but you haven't been very personable."

She stopped typing. "Is that so?"

Olivia sat down at the table. "Yes. You were a completely different person with the girl you interviewed. I was just wondering if this is going to turn out to be a waste of my time."

"I see that you're a very straight-forward person."

"I try to be. There's no need in me coming here when I get off work if I'm just going to be in your way."

This is 30

"Olivia, I've mentored countless women through Bishop's program. In the beginning, it was something that I was very passionate about. I poured everything I had in those women. I can count on my hand how many women have returned here to give back to this program or even say thank you. "

"Why do you continue to do it?

"That's a very good question. My husband asked me the same thing. I don't know, maybe I think that I will be punished if I stop. I certainly don't want the Bishop to be angry. I don't really have an answer for why I continue to offer myself up."

"With all due respect, you're not offering yourself up. You're very much closed off. In the past, you might have been different. My experience over the last two days was horrible." Olivia laughs.

Dr. Odom covers her face and shares a laugh. "I apologize. Let's start over. You tell me what you need from me and I'll tell you what I need from you."

....

While mentorship can be a blessing for you, never forget to pour back into the people who helped along the way. All relationships should be mutually beneficial. While there are some women who could care less about sowing seeds into another woman, they are countless of others waiting to impact your life. These women are not Google. They are providing you with information that could change your life. Treat them as such. And when it's your turn to give back, be the person to your mentee that you needed when you were searching for a mentor. It's a constant cycle of empowerment. It's a never-ending cycle of women helping women. We need more of that.

Chapter 28

"You only live once, but if you do it right, once is enough."

"You only live once, but if you do it right, once is enough."
Mae West

When was the last time you did something for the first time? Someone coined the phrase, "Young, Wild and Free", but many would argue that true adventure has no age limit. In fact, the lack of adventure, fun and excitement can age us quicker than a drop of DNA from Benjamin Button.

As adults, our zest for adventure is replaced with routine and responsibility. Sure, there's this bangin' lounge downtown open for the taking at any given night. Of course there's always dinner and a movie. I'm not speaking of the typical social opportunity. I'm talking about that adrenaline rush you felt when you first took your hands off the handlebars, while speeding down a steep hill. I'm talking about the wonder twinkling in your eyes while watching a flock of fireflies illuminate a nearby field. I'm talking about dancing the night away under the stars, even though you are already three hours past your curfew. You know, the kind of stuff that once made you feel alive.

How do we reinvent those moments as thirty-something women? There are already so many things that we are already responsible for. There's the two thousand square foot home to clean. We have a baby to nurse or children to nurture. We have a husband to attend to. We have a career to maintain. For me, the key is mapping out my day and sticking to my time management schedule. I break my week down by daily "to-dos". No matter how many deadlines I have approaching, I always, always make a point to add a little spice to my life. I just can't stomach the thought that I

This is 30

was born to go to work, take care of people, pay bills, and get ready to die. Seriously, you have to make time for yourself. You have to purposely add adventure to your list of to-dos.

....

Karen and Sonydra have been friends since they were in their early twenties. Both ladies are approaching their forties, but you wouldn't know it by their zest for life and adventure. Although they have families of their own, it's not out of the ordinary to see Sonydra catching a nap at Karen's house on a Sunday evening. They're old school and their husbands are old school too. They will stay outside for hours and hours drinking beer and listening to music, not really concerned with the women.

One day, Karen and Sonydra decide to sneak to the casino that's three hours away from where they live. They have a love hate relationship with Blackjack. They tell their husbands that they are heading to the mall. Even though the men wouldn't care, it would be too much trouble trying to explain why they were going to the casino to lose all of their money. Once they arrive, they spend the first couple of hours buying ten-dollar jewelry in a store. Then they head to the Blackjack table and lose close to five hundred dollars. Sonydra looks at her watch and realizes that they've been in the casino way too long. It's nearing seven o'clock and they need to get on the road since they have a three-hour drive back home. Karen suggests they try to win their money back before leaving. Sonydra agrees and they spend another two hours jumping from table to table. They lose another two hundred dollars. Sonydra is cussing and fussing on the way to the car. She even cusses out the valet guy because she thinks he took too long to bring the car around. To watch them is to watch a comedy show. It's almost like watching Lucy and Ethel.

Karen isn't the best driver. She has poor vision and she gets sleepy quickly. For the first hour of the trip, Sonydra is on the passenger side of the car creating stories that she can tell her husband about how she spent the money. The road is dark and lonely. Trees line each side, and glowing eyes can be seen in the distance. Karen doesn't notice that Sonydra has stopped talking and fallen asleep. Her eyes are getting heavier and heavier. The women aren't sure how long they both were asleep, but they wake up to a horn and five deer staring at them. Karen slams on breaks without hitting the car in the next lane. Sonydra screams and starts hurling cuss words at the deer.

They decide to stop at a nearby store to get some snacks and an energy drink. When the women walk into the store, people start to stare and point. One guy bursts into a fit of laughter. They look at each other in confusion. Sonydra starts to get angry and ask the man what he's laughing at, using the most unpleasant words possible. Karen tries to stop Sonydra from starting a fight with the man. She takes one look at Sonydra's hair and immediately starts laughing with the people in the store. Karen must have hit the breaks so hard that Sonydra's wig completely turns around on her head. Karen hurriedly pays for the snacks and they bolt out of the store. She doesn't tell Sonydra about her wig until they are safely in the car.

After that, there wasn't any talk of the casino or the money they lost. They laughed about the wig until their stomachs hurt. They laughed about the wig until they made it home that night. Even as time went by, they didn't recall how they lost all of their bill money at the casino. The only memory they have is of the time they almost hit a pack of deer, which sent Sonydra's wig spinning in the opposite direction.

....

It's not about how long you live. It's about how you live. It's about what you do on this earth that will be lasting and memorable. Those two friends live on the edge. They worry about tomorrow when tomorrow comes. We can take a page from their book. With all of the responsibilities that we have, and all of the things that require our attention, sometimes it's okay to throw caution to the wind and live a little. We have an eternity to worry. I challenge you to do something you've never done before. I challenge you to take that trip you been thinking about. Buy that purse you've been eyeing. It's not about spending all of your money and going broke. It's about finding some happiness and adventure while you're here. It's about seizing the day. It's about being who you were before you became who you had to be. Live life with no regrets. Buy the damn purse and go on the damn trip.

Chapter 29

"Being brave enough to be alone frees you up to invite people into your life because you want them and not because you need them."

"Being brave enough to be alone frees you up to invite people into your life because you want them and not because you need them."

-Mandy Hale

Solitude is the state or situation of being alone. Alone is the state of isolation. Unfortunately, we live in an age where entertainment is often at the forefront of everyone's daily agenda. Most people confuse alone with being lonely, when there is a massive difference between the two.

In my high school, college, and late twenties, I needed to be around a lot of people. I absolutely despised being by myself. For one, I had no idea what I would do by myself for an entire day. Going to the movies or out to eat alone was out of the question, and sitting home watching television was like watching paint dry. But boy oh boy things dramatically changed when I got a little growth, maturity and self-awareness under my belt. I was living in Atlanta, the most entertaining city in the South. I didn't have any friends or family to call on, it was just me and this big ole' city to explore. This was the era before iPhone Maps. It was just me, a printed copy of directions from MapQuest, and my white drop-top Mustang. I learned how to feel comfortable sitting at a table in a busy restaurant without feeling *lonely*. I learned how to enjoy being in the moment without wondering if everyone was staring at me, wondering why I was all dressed up with no one to socialize with.

I love a night out with my man and girlfriends just like the next person. I enjoy being around people with great energy. But there's something magical about driving to the beach and watching the scenery in silence. There's something refreshing about slowly devouring a juicy T-bone steak without having to talk in-between bites. There's something harmonious about sitting on my back porch, listening to the bird's chirp and the wind whisper, while penning a blog or collection of thoughts.

Being alone doesn't mean you are lonely. Being alone is a place where grown folks frequent. It's a place where the purpose-filled souls live. It's a place where you can drown out the noise and focus on you. It's a place where God speaks, and it's a place where I can hear Him.

....

Erin cleared the table for the hundredth time today. The party that was just seated was obnoxious, needy, and messy. She was so happy when they finished their dinner and exited the restaurant. She closed out the check, winced at the four-dollar tip they left her, and proceeded to greet her next guest.

The woman was strikingly beautiful. She was very well dressed and she had the best posture Erin had ever seen. The woman was mysterious. Being a waitress, Erin often played a little mind game with herself. She would conjure up stories about the people she served. She would envision what their lives were like. She wondered if they were happy or if they were sad. She thought about what they did for a living. She wondered if they had enough love in their lives. Through conversation, she would get some of these questions answered. Some guests were too private or not very talkative. She wouldn't push the conversation forward. She only talked to those who felt like talking to her, mostly men.

Erin sat a chilled glass of water on the table. She sat down two menus and asked the lady if she would care for a glass of wine or something a little stronger until her guest arrived. The woman informed Erin that she will be dining alone and that a glass of wine would be a perfect starter. Erin embarrassingly picked up the extra menu and retreated to the bar. In all her twenty-one years, she hadn't run across a woman who purposely dined alone. The bartender caught her staring at the woman's table.

"Oh, she's a great tipper. Be sure to keep her glass topped off. She comes in here all of the time. She's some big shot reporter or something. She's married with a couple of kids, but I've never seen them in here with her."

"Really? I've never seen a woman come into a restaurant, totally decked out and eat by herself."

"We don't have a lot of them that come in here and do that, but she's definitely a regular. Husband must be an asshole, kids must be brats, and maybe she doesn't have any friends."

Erin thinks about that for a second. "Nah, I think she just enjoys eating by herself. Come to think of it, maybe I should start taking some time to go out by myself. Its kind of badass."

The bartender rolls his eyes. "Here we go with this Beyoncé, Lemonade crap."

Erin laughs. "It's not that deep dude. I mean, sometimes it's tough finding someone to take you out. I've sat home a many night because I didn't have a date. It's nice to see that going out by yourself is an option. I honestly never thought about going to dinner by myself. I felt that I needed someone to be at the table with me."

Erin took the lady a glass of wine and watched her from afar. She didn't look lonely at all. She looked...peaceful.

There's a huge difference in being lonely and being alone. Society would lead us to believe that we need some sort of entertainment to have a good time. I would beg to differ. I'm actually enjoying a dish of Chicken Panang at a local Thai restaurant while I'm typing this chapter. I'm not lonely. I'm being productive, I'm enjoying my food, and I'm very much entertained.

This is 30

Our minds are always racing. There's always some fire to put out. We're in charge of so many things. So many people are counting on us to save the day. It's nice to unplug from it all. The next time that you have the desire to put on your best dress and go out of the town for a bite to eat, I challenge you to go alone. The next time a blockbuster comes out and you're dying to see it, I challenge you to go alone. It feels good to be in the skin I'm in. It feels even better to be comfortable with just being me, even if it's a party of one.

Chapter 30

"There's a level of maturity, confidence, and sexiness that comes with age thirty. You have a little more spunk about yourself. You're not as financially irresponsible as you were. You have a little more ambition, and a whole lot of vision for your life."

This is 30

"There's a level of maturity, confidence, and sexiness that comes with age thirty. You have a little more spunk about yourself. You're not as financially irresponsible as you were. You have a little more ambition, and a whole lot of vision for your life."

-Candace R. McClendon

Turning thirty can be a little intimidating. Especially if you are not where you want to be in life. Or maybe it's not about where you want to be and more of where you thought you'd be. Remember, our biggest problem is comparing who we really are to who we thought we would be when we were young girls. At some point, you have to accept who you are, take responsibility for the mistakes that you've made, and push for a better tomorrow. I think we should do more celebrating in our thirties. I don't know about your twenties, but my twenties were insane. If I could survive some of those days, I think that calls for a celebration.

If you are reading this book and you are not in your thirties, congratulations! You have the opportunity to change some parts of yourself before they become mistakes and regrets. I honestly wouldn't change anything about my journey. People get a little confused when they hear that statement. I'm not implying that I welcome death and pain into my life. I'm simply stating that death and pain have taught me so much about who I am. Who would have thought that I could survive some of the things I've been through? If you would have told me three years ago that I could walk around this earth without my dad, I would have laughed in your face. He meant everything to me. If you would have told me that I would go through 31 weeks of being pregnant, feel my son move around in my body everyday, have to endure thirty-three hours of labor, and then turn around and bury him four days later; I would have laughed in your face. I'm still trying to figure out how God pulled me out of that one. I definitely cannot take full credit for my growth. I'm convinced that although my father is not walking round this earth, he's definitely sitting on my shoulders.

There's no fictional character to accompany this quote. This is the part where you incorporate yourself into each story that was told. This is where you figure out how you can use each principle/story to enhance your life. This is the time for you to reflect on what being 30 means to you? What will you do differently? What are some steps you can take to be a better you?

There are some principles that I tried to echo throughout each chapter:

1. You have to wake up and decide that you want to change for YOU.
2. Success won't work unless YOU do.
3. A person cannot and will not love you better than YOU can love yourself.
4. Every relationship must be mutually beneficial.
5. Worry about today instead of focusing on tomorrow.
6. Enjoy your now.
7. Find inspiration in everyday things.
8. Live on purpose.
9. Grow through what you go through.
10. Control your thoughts.

I'm convinced that joy is on the other side of growth. I am enjoying being thirty-something. I'm grateful for every twist and turn that brought me to this moment in my life. Remember, somebody out there needs what you have. Had I not gone through the things that I have, this book would not be possible. Do you see how that works? When we trust our journey, amazing things can happen as a result of it.

As women, we are constantly trying to navigate our way through life and find that blissful, mind-blowing happiness. After many years of trial and error, I have realized that I already have the secret sauce, and so do you. We just have to tap into it. It won't be easy. It won't be an overnight thing. But it can happen.

Made in the USA
Lexington, KY
13 January 2017